SKYDIVIN

SKYDIVING BASICS
A Parachute Training Manual

Doug Peacock and Andy Allman

PARACHUTE TRAINING SERVICES
ABINGDON 1996

First published 1996
Parachute Training Services 11 Godwyn Close Abingdon
Oxon OX14 1BU

British Library Cataloguing in Publication Data

Data available

ISBN 0-9525825-0-3

Typeset by SetAll (Clifton Hampden, Oxon.)

Printed by J. W. Arrowsmith Ltd.

There is no such thing as failure. There are only results.

Anthony Robbins
Unlimited Power

Contents

List of Figures

Introduction

This handbook is for the student parachutist who wants to learn to jump with safety and precision. It is essentially concerned with the Ram Air Progression System (RAPS) as the serious student will certainly wish to use a modern advanced canopy at the earliest possible opportunity.

Sport jumping in this country has come a long way since the British Parachute Club opened its doors at Fairoaks in 1956, with a handful of students taking turns to hurl themselves backwards from the wing of the Tiger Moth at 1500 feet above the Surrey countryside. Through its Clubs and Centres, the British Parachute Association (BPA) now operates a well-established training system which has progressively evolved over the past thirty years.

This traditional system, utilising a steerable round canopy, has now been updated with the introduction of the Ram Air Progression System for student jumpers. The RAPS student can master the basics of freefall through conventional and well-proven training methods, but will be using a ram-air canopy throughout, bringing an entire new dimension to the operation. As an added safety feature, the parachute opening height is increased to 3,000 feet AGL.

Ram-air, or square, parachutes have been with us since the late 1960s and were originally developed in the United States by Paraflite Inc. of Pennsauken, New Jersey. Rectangular in shape and aerofoil in section, these high-performance canopies were first jumped in the UK in 1971 and for a long time were the prerogative of experienced jumpers only; now they have been modified and rendered sufficiently docile for student use.

The Ram Air Progression System in this country was pioneered in 1986 by Dave Howerski at Swansea Airport and has since been adopted by the Army

Parachute Association as the sole training method at all its Centres worldwide. RAPS is uniquely suited to UK weather conditions where cloudbase is often a limiting factor, and enjoys the following advantages over traditional round canopy progression:

Higher permissible surface windspeeds
Softer landings
Continuity in drills and equipment

In essence, this means that you, the student jumper, will spend less time waiting around for winds to come within limits and will thus make more jumps in the early stages. Coupled with an increased exit height of 3,000 feet, a controlled gliding flight and precision landing, it all adds up to much more fun and a higher retention rate in the Sport.

(Now a brief aside to our women readers. Most of the references in this manual are masculine, but please don't think we're anti-feminist. It's simply that to keep on writing 'he and she' or 'him and her' every time makes for clumsy reading. Approximately one-third of all student jumpers in the UK are women and are accorded absolutely equal respect by these authors).

The Organisation

Sport Parachuting in the United Kingdom is regulated by the Civil Aviation Authority (CAA), and is directly controlled by the British Parachute Association. The BPA started life in 1959 as the Parachute Committee of the Royal Aero Club and became formally recognised as the British Parachute Association in 1961. The first Chairman of this Association was Mike Reilly who was tragically drowned early the following year after parachuting into the English Channel whilst making a film.

Mike was succeeded as Chairman by Colonel Dare Wilson who held the office until 1966. Dare Wilson was the right man at the right time for the fledgling Sport; his legacy is a sound organisation and the drafting of the Basic Safety Regulations which underpin the whole structure of the Association today.

The Royal Aero Club links are still in place. It is through the Royal Aero Club that the Association is affiliated to the Fédération Aéronautique Internationale. The FAI is the world governing body of all aviation sport, and through the International Parachuting Commission (IPC) is responsible for organising all World Parachuting Championships.

The BPA is run by an elected Council and a secretariat with a Technical Officer and a National Coach. There are three sub-committees of Council: Safety and Training, Competitions, and Development. The Safety and Training Committee consists of all Club Chief Instructors (CCIs) and meets every six weeks. As its name suggests, the STC is primarily responsible for the technical control of the Sport in all its aspects and it is the work of this committee that will inform this text. Reference will be made throughout to the 1994 Operations Manual as amended to date.

Operations (Section 1)

The operational conditions under which Sport Parachuting may take place are laid down quite categorically in Section 1 of the Manual—Conduct and Control of Sport Parachuting—which states:

All parachuting within Clubs, Schools, Centres, Associations or Organisations (Clubs) affiliated to the BPA must take place under the following conditions:

(a) Under arrangements made by a BPA Advanced Instructor who is the appointed Club Chief Instructor (CCI) and who is normally present, on a daily basis, when parachuting is taking place

(b) By parachutists with a current Medical Declaration/Certificate who are trained, equipped, and briefed to undertake the planned descent

(c) When an adequate Ground Control organisation is in progress

(d) With an Authorised Pilot and a Jumpmaster who is qualified to take charge of the parachutists on board the aircraft

(e) With parachute equipment in good condition, correctly packed, well fitted and checked before emplaning

(f) From an aircraft that is correctly documented, suitably equipped and prepared for parachuting

(g) When weather conditions are suitable

(h) Onto an approved Dropping Zone (DZ)

(i) With all documentation in order and up to date

(j) According to the conditions laid down in the BPA Operations Manual

(k) When the Club is in possession of a valid Civil Aviation Authority (CAA) Sport Parachuting Permission and Exemption

These basic conditions for the conduct and control of the Sport are your guarantee as a student jumper that your introduction to, and progress in, the Sport will be conducted in a safe and proper manner.

The designation and classification of parachutists (Section 2)

Parachutists are designated as follows:

(a) Student Parachutist — Below Category 8

(b) Parachutist — Category 8 and above, and below FAI 'C' Certificate

(c) Experienced Parachutist — Category 10 and FAI 'C' Certificate

FAI (British Standard) Certificate
'A' Certificate Category 3 or AFF level 3
'B' Certificate Category 5 or AFF level 5
'C' Certificate Category 10, 50 descents and cleared for spotting; has received instruction in the responsibilities of being a jumpmaster
'D' Certificate Category 10, 200 descents

Your training will be conducted by a BPA Approved or Advanced Instructor. He may be assisted by a Basic

Instructor who will be working for his rating under supervision. The higher standards dictated by the RAPS programme require that the student/instructor ratio does not exceed 12–1.

Instructors are qualified as follows:

Approved   The Instructor qualification is particularly stringent; each candidate for the 5-day Basic course will have made a minimum of 200 descents, be qualified to FAI D certificate standard and have been in the Sport for a minimum of two years. Following his Basic Instructor course, the candidate will then be required to spend a minimum further six months working under the direct supervision of his CCI before attending an examination course. On successful completion of the exam course he will be awarded Approved Instructor status and will then be qualified to coach/instruct Student Parachutists up to Category 8.

Advanced   An Advanced Instructor will have spent a minimum of three years as an Approved Instructor, have made at least 1,000 descents and be display and night jump qualified. He must then attend a one week assessment course and may then be recommended to attend a further course for final upgrading.

Examiners   An Examiner will have been an Advanced Instructor for at least two years and must attend at least two Basic Instructor courses in a supervisory capacity for assessment purposes. In order to maintain currency, an Examiner is required to attend an Instructor course at least once every two years.

Club Chief Instructor (CCI)   A CCI will be at least a BPA Advanced Instructor, who is responsible for ensuring that all parachuting, training, and flying activities are carried out in accordance with the Operations Manual. The CCI is principally answerable to the BPA for all matters concerning safety within the Club. Basic Instructor courses and Examination courses are held four times a year at selected Clubs and Centres throughout the UK. These courses are supervised by the BPA Technical Officer and the National Coach who are in turn assisted by a number of Examiners.

About this book

The aim of this handbook is to provide a reference manual, both as an adjunct to your basic course and to expand on the briefings you will be given throughout your progression. Chapters One and Two will examine the basic sport parachute course, and discuss the subjects covered. Chapters Three and Four will deal with the jumping phase and try to advise constructively on some of the problems encountered at various stages in freefall.

One of the main advantages of RAPS is that a high degree of landing accuracy can quickly be achieved and this subject will be covered in Chapter Five. Chapter Six discusses the art and science of spotting.

Your first goal is to achieve Category 8. This can be done by means of the Ram Air Progression System, given reasonable continuity, in about 30–40 descents. You will then come off Student status and be designated as a Parachutist. This qualifies you to make unsupervised solo descents, having demonstrated the ability to perform alternate 360 degree turns, a backloop, a short track and a track turn as an avoidance manoeuvre from a minimum altitude of 8,000 feet AGL.

This last jump is your Cat 8 qualifying dive, and should be given an aerial critique. Once this has been signed up you should be looking forward to Formation Skydiving (FS), which means flying in contact with or in close proximity to other jumpers. Categories 9 and 10 are concerned with the development and refinement of your newly-acquired freefall skills to enable you to achieve this.

Category 9 involves working one-on-one with an instructor and learning to control both fall-rate and horizontal movement. Your Category 10 jumps will introduce you to three-way Formation Skydiving, progressing to four-way and you will qualify by completing four points in a four-way Formation Skydive.

Categories 9 and 10 are now usually achieved through the Worldwide Approved Relativework Progression (WARP) system which has been with us since about 1985, or by the more recently introduced Skydive University 100 programme. Your CCI will be pleased to advise you.

GO FOR IT

1

The Basic Course
Part One

Your introduction to the Sport will be by means of a
Basic Parachute Course, run by a BPA Approved or
Advanced Instructor. As a RAPS student, you will be
in a small group of no more than twelve persons
(Operations Manual Section 5.3). The course will follow a syllabus laid down in the Instructors Manual
and will be of a minimum six hours duration. Because
of the higher skill levels involved in flying a high-performance parachute, this initial training is likely to be
extended to at least eight hours. You will not be
allowed to jump until the instructor is satisfied with
your ability to make your first descent in complete
safety. Progression beyond the first descent is by
means of a graduated series of jumps from higher altitudes involving longer freefalls, each jump being critiqued by your instructor. This progression is covered
in greater detail in Chapters 3 and 4. The basic course
will cover the following subjects.

Orientation and Documentation
Familiarisation with equipment
Fitting equipment
After landing procedures
Ram-air landings and parachute landing falls
Basic stability
Aircraft exits and aircraft drills
Emergency aircraft drills
Aerodynamics of the canopy
Canopy control and flight drills
The reserve parachute
Malfunctions and reserve drills

References throughout the text are to the relevant section in the Operations Manual.

Lesson One: Orientation and Documentation

Orientation

This will consist of an introductory lecture, outlining the background to Sport Parachuting in general and the Centre in particular. The basic safety regulations and the training syllabus will be explained. This lecture will be followed by a walk around the Dropping Zone and you will be briefed on any special features and hazards. You will also be briefed on airfield discipline and any local safety regulations.

Documentation (Section 12)

The necessary initial documentation consists of a training record card, a medical declaration of fitness to parachute, and student provisional membership of the British Parachute Association. Most Centres have their own training record cards, which also have space for recording the first few descents. As progress is made, descents must be entered in a Parachutists Log Book (Section 12.1. (e)). The minimum age for parachuting in the UK is 16. Persons over the age of 50 are not normally accepted for training unless they have previous parachuting experience or can demonstrate exceptional fitness to the instructor (Section 11).

Medical Declaration (Section 11) You must complete a medical declaration of fitness to parachute, which must be signed by yourself and witnessed. In the case of a jumper under the age of 18, the witness must be the parent or guardian. If you are over 40 years of age, or are uncertain about a medical condition or previous injury, the certificate must be countersigned and stamped by a doctor. The medical declaration is shown at Figure 1.1.

BPA Membership BPA student provisional membership is mandatory. This is valid for a period of twelve months, or until you progress on to freefall. In the case of a jumper under 18 the membership agreement must be countersigned by the parent or guardian. BPA membership gives insurance cover which indemnifies members against claims by third parties to a current (1995) maximum of £1,000,000.

Lesson Two: Familiarisation with Equipment (Section 6).
Fitting Equipment

Personal equipment

This normally consists of a one-piece jumpsuit, a student Protec helmet and an altimeter. In cold weather it is advisable to wear thin leather gloves (aircrew type). For the modern student, the most suitable footwear is training shoes, the days of the big paratroop boots are now long gone. If you wear contact lenses, goggles are advised; if you wear spectacles, they should be of the sport type or be retained behind the head with an elastic band. For freefall jumpers, goggles are advised anyway for delays in excess of ten seconds. Student radios are mandatory for the first three descents. As a RAPS jumper you should also be wearing an altimeter to assist you in canopy control, although this is an optional extra. Altimeters are normally either chest- or wrist-mounted. They are delicate instruments and should not be subjected to rough usage. The most common in the UK are the Altimaster II and III, manufactured in New Jersey by SSE Inc. (see Glossary).

BRITISH PARACHUTE ASSOCIATION LTD
5 Wharf Way, Glen Parva, Leicester, LE2 9TF
Tel: 0116 278 5271
Fax: 0116 247 7662

DECLARATION OF FITNESS TO PARACHUTE

I hereby declare that I am physically fit. I do not, and have not suffered from any of the following conditions which I understand may lead to a dangerous situation with regard to myself or other persons during parachuting:

Epilepsy, fits, severe head injury, recurrent blackouts or giddiness, disease of the brain or nervous system, high blood pressure, heart or lung disease, recurrent weakness or dislocation of any limb, diabetes, mental illness, drug or alcohol addiction.

I further declare that in the event of contracting or suspecting any of the above conditions, or in the event of sickness absence over twenty consecutive days, incapacitating injury or confirmation of pregnancy, I will cease to parachute until I have obtained medical approval. I have read the notes overleaf.

Name in CAPITALS   Date of Birth   Weight

Signature   BPA Number   Height

Signature of Witness   Name of Witness in CAPITALS   Date
(for parachutists under 18 years of age, the Witness MUST be the parent or guardian)

= =

IF YOU CANNOT SIGN THE DECLARATION BECAUSE OF ANY OF THE ABOVE CONDITIONS, OR IF YOU ARE AGED 40 OR MORE, YOU MUST OBTAIN THE DOCTORS CERTIFICATE BELOW BEFORE PARACHUTING.

= =

DOCTOR'S CERTIFICATE

I understand that the applicant wishes to parachute but is unable to sign the above declaration/aged 40 or over*. I have read the notes overleaf. In my opinion the applicant is physically and mentally capable of parachuting. Glasses or contact lenses must/need not* be worn.

Signature

Date of Signature   Date of Expiry

*Delete as applicable   (Doctor's Stamp)

Form 114 (i)

Figure 1.1 (*and over*) Declaration of fitness to parachute

NOTES FOR PARACHUTISTS Parachutists need a reasonably high standard of physical fitness and must not be overweight in relation to their sex, age, and height. No person above the age of 50 years will normally be accepted for novice parachute training. Exceptions to this rule may be allowed if the candidate either has previous experience or is of a high standard of fitness and can convince the instructor of that fitness.

As well as the conditions listed overleaf, the following may cause problems to parachutists and if you have ever suffered from any of them you must seek medical approval before parachuting:

Previous fractures, back strain, arthritis and severe joint sprains. Chronic bronchitis. Asthma. Rheumatic fever. Pneumothorax. Liver or Kidney disease. Thyroid, adrenal or other glandular disorder. Chronic ear or sinus disease. Any condition which requires the regular use of drugs. Anaemia. Recent blood donation.

If you wear spectacles they should be securely attached while parachuting. If contact lenses are used, protective goggles should be worn. Your sight must be adequate to read a car number plate at 25 yards.

NOTES FOR DOCTORS Cardiorespiratory fitness is important. Sport parachutists make descents from unpressurised aircraft at heights of 2,200 to 15,500 feet above sea level without supplementary oxygen. At 15,000 feet there is a 40% reduction in available oxygen. A tachycardia of 120 - 160 bpm is common in experienced parachutists and 200 bpm is not unusual in novices. The tachycardia may be present at the same time as relative hypoxia and considerable physical exertion.

Musculoskeletal fitness is required. The parachutist must be able to operate his equipment with either hand and should be able to exert a pull of 30 lbs with either hand in any direction. During the parachute deployment there is a brisk deceleration, usually about 4g but occasionally up to 5g. The landing impact typically involves a descent rate equivalent to jumping from a wall 4 feet high, with a horizontal speed of 0-15 mph. Occasionally the landing impact may be greater than this. Pre-existing spinal or joint injuries may be exacerbated. Obesity increases the likelihood of lower limb or spinal injuries.

A visual acuity of at least 6/12 (after correction with spectacles or contact lenses) is required. Blindness in one eye is acceptable providing that the remaining eye has a full field and the candidate has adapted to monocular vision. Middle ear or sinus disease may cause problems due to the rapid changes in ambient air pressure. The rate of descent in freefall may exceed 10,000 ft/min and under an open canopy 1,000 ft/min. Normal peripheral sensation and coordination are required to activate the parachute but may be impaired by disorders of the nervous system or peripheral vasculature. On early jumps the candidate is responsible mainly for his own safety but must behave in such a way as to cause no hazard to others. After further training, but no further medical evidence, the candidate may be the sole person responsible for the safety of an aircraft full of student parachutists. The candidate must be physically and psychologically fit to carry this responsibility.

The following conditions will normally make a candidate UNFIT to parachute, although there are some exceptions: Any condition which can lead to blackouts, impaired consciousness or impaired concentration. Tendency to persistent or recurrent weakness or dislocation of any limb (unless successfully corrected by surgery). Conditions requiring the use of medication with sedative or psychotropic side effects. A history of ischemic heart disease, uncontrolled hypertension, other significant cardiac or respiratory disease, cerebrovascular disease, epilepsy, diabetes, mental illness, drug addition, alcohol dependence, significant CNS disease. In cases of doubt, or where further information is required, the Medical Adviser to the British Parachute Association or the National Coach and Safety Officer will be pleased to help, and may be contacted at the address overleaf.

These notes are not exhaustive. Some candidates who are "unfit" using the above criteria may still be fit to make a tandem parachute descent (strapped into a common harness with an experienced instructor) - see separate "Student Tandem Parachutist" form.

VALIDITY The parachutists declaration overleaf places the parachutist under a permanent obligation to cease parachuting until obtaining a doctors approval if he develops any of the listed conditions. It is valid up to the age of 40. Doctors certificates are valid as follows:

Age under 50 years	-	24 months
Age 50 - 70 years	-	12 months
Age over 70 years	-	6 months

provided that the examining doctor can specify a shorter period of validity if he/she feels it appropriate.

Form 114 (ii)

Figure 1.1

The parachute

Container and harness   The most important item of equipment, naturally, is the parachute. All parachutists making a premeditated descent (as opposed to an emergency bailout) within the United Kingdom are to be equipped with a minimum of two airworthy parachutes on a common harness (Section 6.1). Static line RAPS equipment consists of a piggyback assembly (see Glossary) with a static-line operated main parachute in the lower half of the container and a manually operated reserve parachute in the top half. The assembly can also be converted for use in the freefall mode. The equipment must be fitted with an automatic activation device (AAD) and a reserve static line (RSL). A typical RAPS assembly is shown in Figure 1.2.

The main canopy   The main canopy must be 'docile' (Section 6.2). In practice this usually means a large (288 sq ft) 9-cell ram-air canopy with a typical maximum all-up weight loading of 275lb. For lighter weight jumpers sometimes a smaller 200 sq ft canopy is used. Such canopies have an airspeed range of approximately 5 to 20mph. For a full description of the student ram-air canopy see Figure 1.3 and Chapter 2.

The reserve canopy   This may be either a conventional round canopy or a ram-air canopy. If the latter it should also be appropriately 'docile'. Round reserve canopies are typically aeroconical in shape, steerable, with a forward speed of some 5–8mph and a descent rate of 18–20fps. At the time of writing, there are no real objections to a round reserve canopy in a RAPS assembly and indeed there can be some strong arguments in its favour. A typical round reserve canopy is illustrated in Figure1.4. Use of the reserve parachute will be discussed further in Lesson 9.

The Reserve Static Line (RSL)   This is sometimes referred to as the Stevens Lanyard, after its American inventor. It consists of a short (18″) lanyard attached

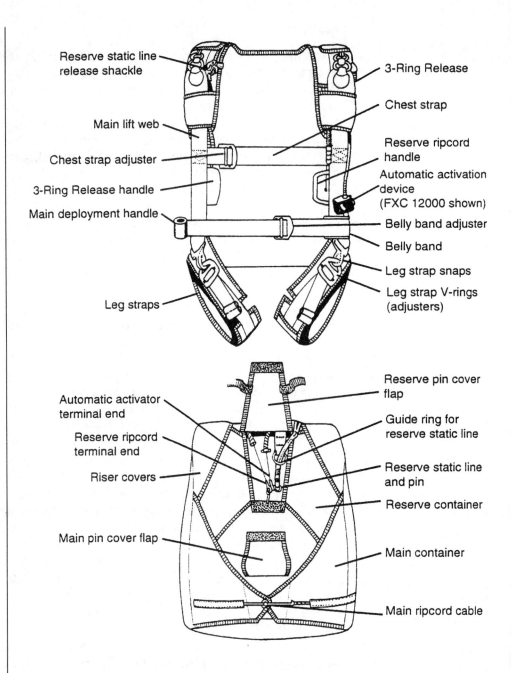

Reserve static line release shackle

3-Ring Release

Chest strap

Main lift web

Reserve ripcord handle

Chest strap adjuster

Automatic activation device (FXC 12000 shown)

3-Ring Release handle

Main deployment handle

Belly band adjuster

Belly band

Leg strap snaps

Leg strap V-rings (adjusters)

Leg straps

Reserve pin cover flap

Automatic activator terminal end

Guide ring for reserve static line

Reserve ripcord terminal end

Riser covers

Reserve static line and pin

Reserve container

Main pin cover flap

Main container

Main ripcord cable

Figure 1.2 A RAPS freefall parachute assembly

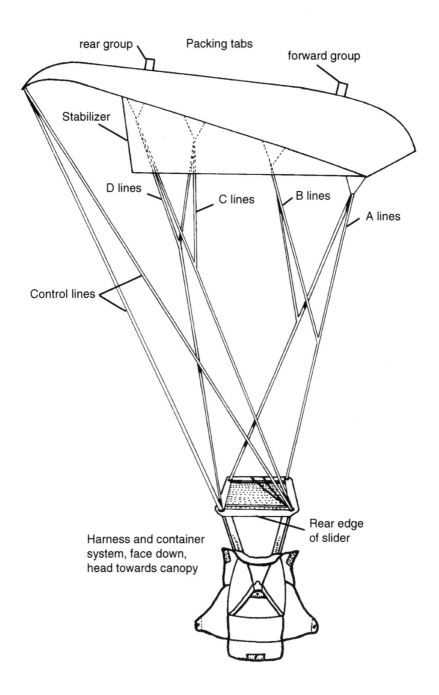

Figure 1.3 The main canopy

Figure 1.4 A
round reserve
canopy

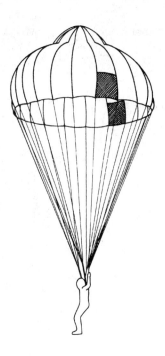

by a shackle to one set of main risers at one end and to
the reserve ripcord cable (or the pin itself) at the other.
The function of the RSL is automatically to deploy the
reserve parachute in the event of the main being cut
away.

The automatic activation device (AAD)

The Operations Manual Section 6.2 (b) requires that
piggyback assemblies be fitted with an AAD. The most
common AADs in use today are the FXC 12000 and the
CYPRES.

It is important to remember that AADs of whatever
type are only in place to back up manual operation
of the reserve, and this point will be considered in
Lesson 9.

The FXC Automatic Parachute Ripcord Release
Model 12000 is manufactured in California by the FXC

Corporation (see Glossary) and is designed to operate the jumper's (reserve) parachute at a pre-set height AGL (normally 1500ft) if, and only if, the descent rate exceeds 40fps. It consists of a barometric altitude-sensing device, coupled with a rate-of-descent sensor; the reserve pin is pulled by a spring-loaded cable. It is important that the FXC is functionally tested at the reserve repack cycle and serviced at the required intervals according to the manufacturer's instructions.

The CYPRES (Cybernetic Parachute Release System) is a smaller, more sophisticated AAD. It was designed and is manufactured in Germany by Airtec GmbH (see Glossary). It consists of an electronic rate-of-descent/altitude sensor and a small pyrotechnic cartridge which fires a guillotine to sever the reserve closure loop at the preset altitude when rate of descent parameters are exceeded.

Handling the parachute

The parachute is a specialised item of lifesaving equipment and must be treated accordingly. It should be stored under controlled conditions of temperature and humidity. It should not be exposed to oil, dirt, or corrosive fluids etc, for example in the boot of a car or back of a Land Rover. It should always be kept in a parabag when in transit. On the DZ, if not being fitted, it should be laid harness down on a packing mat (drag mat) and kept well clear of wet, muddy or oily surfaces. It should not be exposed to strong sunlight for any period of time as UV rays will cause the fabric to deteriorate.

To carry the parachute, either wear it or carry it in both arms. Do not attempt to pick it up by the risers as these may be pulled out of the container.

Look after the parachute and it will look after you

Inspections   Each parachute assembly has a record of inspection, which has to be renewed every six calendar months. Correct maintenance of the parachute is obviously of vital importance and it is preferable that this six-monthly inspection is carried out by a qualified rigger (see Glossary). In addition, a visual check of all components is made every time the parachute is repacked. The reserve parachute is subject to a six-month repack cycle. It is pulled, shaken out, fully inspected and then repacked and the test pull poundage recorded (minimum 5lb, maximum 22lb).

Fitting equipment

The correct fitting of the harness is extremely important as this will materially affect your comfort and safety during freefall, deployment sequence, and the ride down. The parachute harness is designed to be effective and comfortable under an open canopy and it thus follows that the height adjustment must be correct and the leg straps snugly fitting. As part of the fitting period you should practise a hands-on check of the cutaway pad and the reserve handle.

Safety checks

As a matter of principle, you should carry out the following safety checks every time before putting the parachute on.

Static line assemblies and cable-deployed freefall assemblies:
Back
1. Security of closure loop and free movement of pin/cable
2. Routing and correct stowage of static line
3. Position/accessibility of handle (freefall assembly)
4. Security of closure loop and free movement of pin and cable (reserve)
5. Routing of RSL and power cable of AAD (FXC). Electronic setting (CYPRES)

Front
1. Assembly and security of three-ring release both sides (check teflon cable)
2. RSL shackle security
3. Security and positioning of cutaway pad. Check velcro peel
4. Security and positioning of reserve handle in pocket; free movement of cable in the housing
5. FXC setting

Flight line checks

Once on the flight line, you will be allowed plenty of time to fit the harness before emplaning; all jumpers should be encouraged to work in pairs and help each other. There is nothing worse than rushing around at the last minute before jumping: **If you are in a hurry, you are in danger—stop.** The student flight line check must be carried out by an instructor (Section 1.3).

It is recommended that you fit your parachute at least twenty minutes before emplaning. This will ensure that you are comfortable before the final safety check is carried out by the flight-line checker. This instructor will then systematically carry out all checks detailed in the previous paragraph; security of all buckles and snaphooks is confirmed, altimeters are zeroed, radios are checked, and helmets are secured. Once the flight-line check has been carried out, all jumpers should remain in stick order (see Glossary) in a defined area until emplaning.

Sometimes the flight-line check is carried out by two instructors; in this case they must be absolutely specific about who has and who has not been checked. Therefore, once you have been checked, stay put.

Lesson Three: After-landing Procedures

On the basic course, it is often convenient after the fitting period to demonstrate the deployment sequence of the static line parachute. Once this has been done, the instructor may then use this canopy to demonstrate after-landing procedures and give you practice in carrying these out.

Ram-air canopies normally deflate on landing; if the winds are towards the upper permissible limits, your canopy may remain inflated after you have landed. In this case you must actively deflate the canopy either by running downwind of the canopy or by pulling in on one steering line. If you are being dragged and cannot regain your feet, you must take the latter option and deflate the canopy by pulling in one steering line to the maximum extent.

You should deflate a round canopy either by getting up onto your feet and running downwind or, in the case of dragging, by rolling over onto your front and pulling in on one lower set of suspension lines until the canopy collapses.

To collapse the canopy of a jumper who is being dragged and cannot help himself, simply catch hold of the stabilizer panel and pull the canopy into wind. Alternatively pull in one steering line as outlined above.

Once the canopy is fully deflated, stand up and hank up the suspension lines, letting the slider drop down the lines toward the stabilizer panels. This should be done neatly, while walking towards the canopy. Do not drag the canopy along the ground. Take care also to avoid getting tangles in the lines at this stage, as this will only mean extra work for the subsequent packer—who might be you. Then gather up the canopy prior to leaving the DZ for the packing area.

Keep your helmet on at all times and pay particular attention to aircraft movements and other jumpers when leaving the landing area.

Field Packing

Once in the packing area, place the canopy on the ground and walk backward to full line stretch before taking off the harness and laying the container (harness down) on the drag mat. Bring the slider down to the connector links. Then grasp the rear suspension lines, including the brake lines, with the right hand and the front set with the left hand above the slider. Now walk towards the canopy, shake it out and lay it down. This will orientate the canopy on its right side with the nose to the left and the tail to the right. Then straighten the lines by applying tension.

The procedure is then to kneel at the top of the canopy facing down the lines and fold the nose into the centre using two or three folds. Keeping tension on the lines, repeat the procedure to fold the tail on top of the folded nose section. The canopy should now be in a tubular shape approximately 18″ wide. This is then rolled up until the lines are reached.

The lines may then either be daisy-chained or loosely hanked into the packtray. Rolling the canopy up the lines is not recommended for the beginner as this all too often leads to monumental tangles if not done properly. Once the lines are in the packtray, place the canopy on top of the lines and hand the assembly back into the store in optimum configuration for the next repack.

Lesson Four: Ram-air Landings and Parachute Landing Falls

On a RAPS course, two types of landing are taught; first, how to land the main canopy and second, how to make a parachute landing fall if for any reason the landing speed/attitude requires it.

Landing a ram-air canopy

It is axiomatic that all landings are made into wind to minimise ground speed. Make the final turn into wind no lower than 500ft, on half or three-quarter brakes (see Lesson 8 on **Canopy Control**). At a height no lower than 100ft, let the brakes full off and fly the canopy at maximum airspeed.

Just before touchdown, at a height of some 10–15ft,

smoothly apply maximum brake. This will cause the canopy to flare, or round out, and you can simply step down on to the ground. This technique is very soon learned and the only caveat is that once full brakes have been finally applied, they must under no circumstances be released. It is also important to remember that the canopy must be flown at full speed prior to braking in order to generate the lift which gives the soft landing.

Parachute landing falls (PLFs)

Parachute landing falls are designed to absorb the vertical and horizontal speeds normally involved in a conventional (round) parachute landing. They are currently taught on RAPS courses, even if both parachutes are of the ram-air variety, on the premise that some landings will inevitably be faster than others and a good PLF will certainly minimise the risk of injury. The most important aspect of a PLF is the initial touchdown position: the feet and knees must be pressed tightly together with the knees slightly bent and the soles of the feet parallel to the ground. The chin should be on the chest with the back rounded and the elbows forward (Figure 1.5). Six directional landings are practised—forwards, sideways, and backwards to the right and the same to the left. You must be able to take any directional landing 360 degrees all around the clock at any speed with complete confidence.

Abnormal or hazardous landings

These are by definition landings outside the Dropping Zone, and could be into:

Trees
Water
Buildings (including roof landings)
Power lines

Rule one, of course, is to avoid missing the Drop Zone in the first place. However, out landings may occur

Figure 1.5 The PLF position

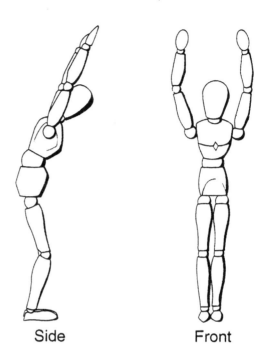

Side   Front

either as the result of a bad spot, bad canopy handling, a reserve ride, or emergency abandonment of the aircraft. Most out landing situations should be obviated by competent jumpmasters, good training and the use of a backup radio; however out landings do occur even in the best regulated circles and you should take the following steps to cope safely with an abnormal landing.

Avoidance Avoid the obstacle if possible, even if this means making a crosswind or a downwind landing.

Trees Go into trees with the feet and knees tight together and the hands crossed to protect the face. If you are treed stay there and wait for assistance.

Water If your DZ is within 1200 metres of a deep river or open water you will be equipped with a flotation aid anyway (Section 7.5). If you know you are going into the water, unhook the RSL shackle and cut your main canopy away as your feet enter the water (not before). Then inflate your buoyancy aid.

Buildings   The safest way to connect with the side of a building is sideways on. All you can do is hold a good parachuting position and keep the elbows well tucked in to the sides. Keep the feet and knees together to prepare for the slide down. If you land on the roof, disconnect the RSL shackle and cut the main canopy away to avoid being dragged off the roof. Stay put until help arrives.

Power lines   This is obviously a particularly hazardous one, and it must be remembered that the normal domestic supply cables of 11kv are potentially lethal. If a landing in power lines is inevitable, try at all costs to avoid touching two cables simultaneously. If your feet are touching the ground, cut away the main canopy, disconnect the RSL shackle and walk away. Leave the gear where it is.

Having discussed hazardous landings, however, it must be remembered that you have a high degree of manoeuvrability with a ram-air canopy and consequently you have every chance of finding a safe landing area even if for any of the aforementioned reasons you have to make an out landing.

Lesson Five: Basic Stability

Let us not forget that the name of the game is freefall parachute jumping. Your initial static line jumps are merely stepping stones placed there for your safety. Before considering the question of stability, let us examine for a moment the forces at work and the speeds involved in freefall.

As the parachutist leaves the aircraft, there are three forces acting on the body—projection, or throw forward; gravity; and air pressure. We will ignore projection for the moment and consider first the effect of gravity. The speed of gravity-induced acceleration in a vacuum is approximately 32ft/sec/sec. We are, however, operating in an atmosphere and a jumper in a full spread position is presenting an area of about 10 square feet to the airflow. Under these conditions the jumper will accelerate for the first 12 seconds of freefall until the balance of gravity and air pressure is reached and the jumper will continue to fall at a terminal velocity (TV) of 174ft/sec in a full spread position. This translates to a speed of 120mph.

As a jumper, it is more relevant for you to consider these speeds in terms of height loss; at TV one thousand feet are lost every six seconds. This is the reason why the minimum opening height in sport jumping is 2,000ft AGL (See Table 1.1.) As a RAPS static line jumper your opening height is 3,000ft, which is comparatively high in sport jumping terms.

With regard to projection, as the jumper leaves the door, he is initially travelling at the same speed as the aircraft. His trajectory is a parabolic curve as he accelerates earthwards under gravity. This throw-forward decays and for all practical purposes ceases after about 10 seconds. The significance of projection will be covered in greater detail in Lesson 6 on **Exits** and further in Chapter 6 (**Spotting**).

Stability

From the very first descent, you will be taught to exit the aircraft and to adopt a stable spread position on the airflow. This is in anticipation of freefall jumping at a later stage. The two most important elements in stability are body curvature and symmetry. First, the curved surface will always face the airflow as the centre of gravity is below the centre of pressure; thus, in order to remain face to earth, all you have to do is arch the back, spread the arms and legs wide, and thrust the hips forward (Figure 1.6).

Secondly, absolute symmetry of the body and limbs is necessary to ensure lateral stability, that is to ensure

Table 1.1: Distance fallen in stable spread position

This table is computed for free fall in the stable spread position (face to earth) for an opening altitude of 2,000 feet AMSL for average pressure conditions. The rate of descent increases with:

(1) Other body position
(2) Lower pressure (eg higher field elevation)

Seconds	Altitude loss per second (feet)	Cumulative altitude loss
1	16	16
2	46	62
3	76	138
4	104	242
5	124	366
6	138	504
7	148	652
8	156	808
9	163	971
10	167	1138
11	171	1309
12	174	1483
15	174	2005
20	174	2875
25	174	3745
30	174	4615
35	174	5485
40	174	6355
45	174	7225
50	174	8095
55	174	8965
60	174	9835

Figure 1.6
Stability: the
forces acting on
the freefalling
jumper

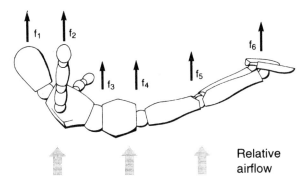

The body in free fall presents an aerodynamic resistance
to the relative airflow.

Each of these forces f_1, f_2, f_3, . . . represents the airflow
resistance to the head, arms and body . . .

The sum of these forces f_1, f_2, f_3, may be represented by
a single force F

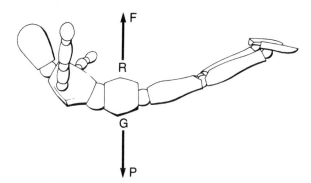

F is equal to the total sum of aerodynamic forces acting
on the body in freefall. Its point of application is the point
R, centre of pressure.

P is the force equal to the weight of the body. Its point of
application is the point G, the centre of gravity of the
individual.

Figure 1.6 illustrates stability: the point of application of F
is above the point of application of weight G. These
forces are now equal and opposite, F = P which explains
why the body will cease to accelerate once it has
reached the terminal velocity of 174ft/sec.

Figure 1.7 The
stable spread
position

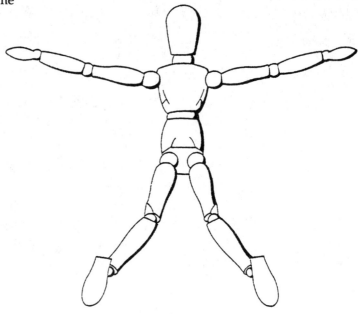

Symmetrical positioning of arms and legs is essential to
maintain lateral stability.

that you maintain a heading throughout the length of
the delay with no involuntary turning (Figure 1.7).
Because even a slight misalignment of arm or leg will
cause a rotation you must learn to present an
absolutely symmetrical curved surface to the airflow.
Variations on the basic stable position are further considered in Chapters 3 and 4 (**The Training
Progression**). What must be mastered first, however, is
the stable face-to-earth position before any progress
can be made.

This position ensures that you can see where you are
going (DOWN) and also allows the main parachute,
on your back, to deploy into clean air and not become
snagged on your limbs or body. On static line jumping,

body attitude on deployment is not quite so critical. Because of the static line bag system in use, you will always get a canopy above your head within two seconds of making an exit.

In freefall, however, a bad position on opening could cause serious deployment problems, hence the insistence on a minimum of five good static line exits, including three consecutive dummy ripcord pulls (DRCPs) before you are allowed to progress to freefall. The first freefall must take place no later than the day following the last of three successful DRCPs. Dummy ripcord pulls and the first freefall will be discussed in detail in Chapter 3.

Lesson Six: Aircraft Exits

The aim of the exit is to launch you onto the airflow outside the door and achieve immediate stability. The method of exit will vary according to the type of aircraft used—right or left hand door, seated exit, poised exit, tailgate exit or whatever. What has to be mastered is the relative airflow.

This airflow on exit is horizontal, and is caused by the forward speed of the aircraft. It follows, therefore, that initial stability must be achieved on this horizontal relative wind before the throw-forward decays and you pick up more vertical speed. It is important that you practise the exit many times from the mock-up, with the emphasis on thrusting the hips forward immediately you are outside the door. You only have one chance to get it right on the jump.

From the side door, either sitting or standing, the exit should be angled into the airflow; from a left hand door you should pivot with the left shoulder forward into the slipstream, vice-versa from a right hand door. This is to avoid peeling left or right on exit as the case may be. In the early stages, the exit should be made hard and with aggression, the hips thrust forward, presenting a good positive arch to the relative wind.

The importance of this dynamic approach cannot be over-emphasised at this stage.

Coupled with the exit is the count. The purpose of the count is first, to measure elapsed time; when you reach Category 6 you will be required accurately to count fifteen seconds freefall time before opening your parachute. The second reason for counting, and counting out loud, is to release the mental and physical tension which will inevitably have built up during the climb to altitude. A typical count is: One thousand, Two thousand, Three thousand, Four thousand, Check Canopy. This count should, of course, take four seconds.

Lesson Seven: Aircraft Drills

This period consists of the introduction to the type of aircraft to be used, including a safety brief covering the following points:

Approaching the aircraft
No smoking near the aircraft
Dangers of foreign object damage (FOD)
Danger from propellers
Danger of interfering with aircraft controls in a
    confined space
Awareness of door handles

For this period, a mock-up of the aircraft can be used. First of all you will practise exits without the encumbrance of a parachute until the instructor is satisfied that you have fully mastered the exit technique. You will then practise aircraft drills with all kit on, either from the same mock-up or from the jump aircraft itself. The object is to familiarise you with the aircraft environment and to act as a rehearsal for the first descent. The following actions will be covered:

Emplaning and hooking up
Seating positions
Pre-jump checks

Jumpmaster positioning and commands
Moving into the door
Static line clearance
Exits.

Emergency aircraft drills

The following emergency situations will be covered:

Engine failure below 1,000ft
Engine failure above 1,000ft
Reserve/main parachute pulled inside aircraft
Hung up parachutist procedure

In an emergency situation it must be emphasised that all commands will come from the jumpmaster, after direction from the pilot. The following procedures must be followed:

Engine failure below 1,000ft   If time permits, switch off FXCs and unhook static lines
Jumpers all face aft and adopt brace position with hands behind the head
As the aircraft comes to rest, door is opened and jumpers exit and clear the area at speed.

Engine failure above 1,000ft   Jumpers remain hooked up and exit in one stick under control of the jumpmaster.

Reserve/main parachute opens inside the aircraft
Nearest jumper concentrates on containing the canopy/extractor parachute to prevent it accidentally going out of the door.
Inform jumpmaster.

Hung up parachutist   A hang up occurs when the static line becomes jammed on some part of the jumper's body or equipment and the pin cannot be withdrawn. This results in the parachutist being towed behind the aircraft. A hang up is avoided by correct stowage of the static line on the container and by correct static line control by the jumpmaster.

As the jumper cannot be retrieved into the aircraft in this situation, the following drills are put into operation:

- The aircraft climbs to 4,000ft
- Jumper places both hands on helmet. This is a signal to the jumpmaster that the student is aware of the situation, and also ensures that the student does not pull his reserve prematurely while still connected to the aircraft . . .
- Jumper is cut free by jumpmaster
- Jumper immediately deploys reserve parachute.

In conclusion, remember that time spent on aircraft drills is time very well spent. Most jump aircraft are pretty cramped with a full load on board and it is important that you are prepared for this factor. The jumpmaster will try to keep movement to a minimum, and for your part you must be aware of the need to keep reserve handles and cutaway pads guarded and ensure that all static lines are kept clear and running freely down the cable. Constant practise on the ground will ensure a smooth and safe performance in the air from all concerned.

2

The Basic Course
Part Two

So far, all we have considered is a basic parachute course, with little or no mention of the type of canopy we shall be using. Part 2 of the course will concentrate on the aerodynamics of the ram-air canopy, the flight drills and canopy control techniques, and considerations of drift. Finally we shall look at the reserve parachute in more detail and discuss malfunctions of the main canopy and reserve drills.

Introduction: The Aerodynamics of the Ram-air Canopy

The essential difference between a conventional (round) canopy and a ram-air (square) canopy is that the former is a drag device and the latter is a lift device. The forward speed of the ram-air canopy is generated through the interaction of gravity and the angle of incidence (see Glossary) of the canopy (Figure 2.1). The canopy is constructed in an aerofoil shape and the pressure differential thus created between the upper and lower surfaces gives the canopy lift. The ram-air parachute is a non-rigid glider and must be controlled as such.

Canopy deployment

On deployment air is rammed into the open cells at the nose and because the fabric is virtually non-porous (0–3cfm) these cells remain pressurised. Equal pressurisation across the whole span is effected by

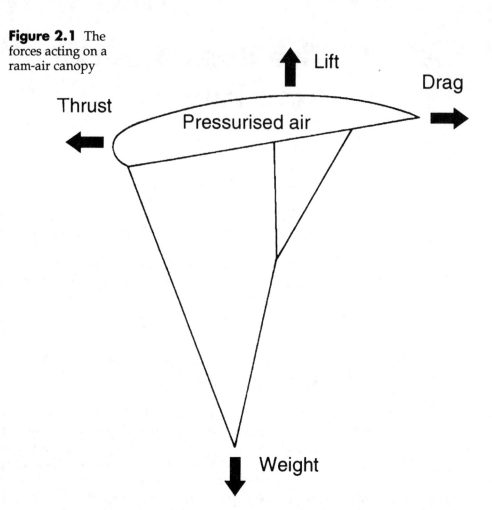

Figure 2.1 The forces acting on a ram-air canopy

cross-port venting (see Glossary). It is important to realise that this is a very fast-opening canopy and the action of the slider is essential to reduce opening shock to an acceptable level. The nose, being cut square, is not an efficient leading edge; the true leading edge is formed by the bubble of air forced out of the cells at the nose by internal air pressure (Figure 2.2). This is the point at which the relative airflow (see Glossary) is deflected over the upper and lower surfaces of the canopy to create the pressure differential illustrated in Figure 2.3.

Figure 2.2 Cell pressurisation within a ram-air canopy

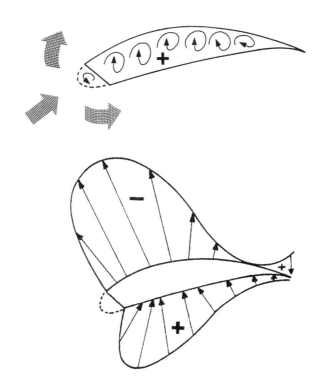

Figure 2.3 The pressure differential on the upper and lower surfaces of the aerofoil

Lesson Eight: Canopy Control and Flight Drills

The canopy is controlled by means of toggles connected to brake lines which are attached to the trailing edge of the canopy (Figure 2.4). The toggles, positioned on the rear of the rear risers, control the forward speed and rate of descent of the canopy and are used to turn the canopy. These control effects are discussed below.

Brakes

The canopy is flying at maximum airspeed when the brakes are off, that is the arms are extended and there is no tension on the toggles. This airspeed, in a typical student canopy, is about 20mph. Half brakes (Figure

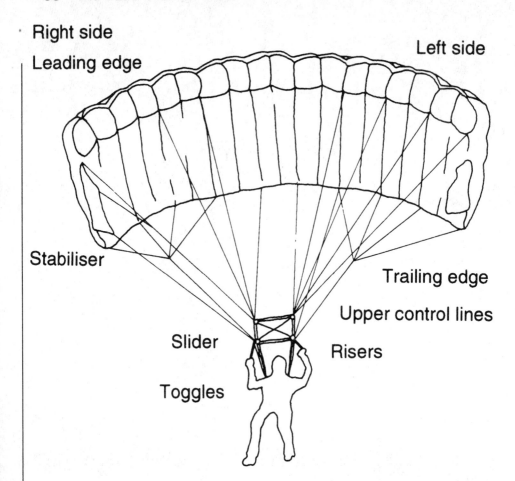

Right side

Left side

Leading edge

Stabiliser

Trailing edge

Upper control lines

Slider

Risers

Toggles

Figure 2.4 A nine cell canopy showing control line attachments

2.5a) is achieved by pulling both toggles down to just above waist level. This will slow the canopy down to approximately 10mph (airspeed remember) and at the same time will generate increased lift because of a larger effective wing section. Full brakes is both toggles pulled down to arms length (Figure 2.5b). In this configuration the canopy has an airspeed of about 5mph and is thus barely maintaining flying speed. Further depression of the brakes will result first in a sink and then a stall (Figure 2.5c). It is important to remember that the canopies you as a student will be using have brake settings such that they cannot be stalled. The canopy is flown throughout the descent in varying brake modes according to the circumstances and the briefing (see **Flight Drills**).

Turning the canopy

Turns are achieved by differential application of brake. To turn right, pull the right toggle, to turn left, pull the left one. A full glide turn is made by depressing one toggle fully and leaving the other one at the keeper. Such turns will encompass a wide arc due to the high

Figure 2.5a
The canopy on
half brakes

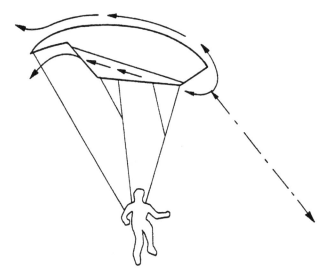

Figure 2.5b
The canopy on
full brakes

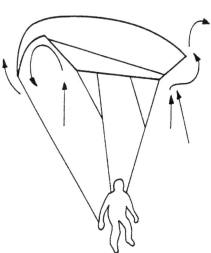

Figure 2.5c The canopy in a stalled condition

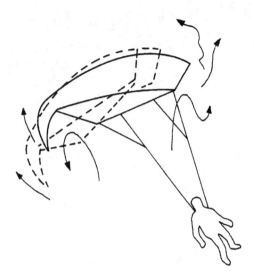

forward speed; the canopy will bank and the loss of lift thus entailed will result in an increased rate of descent. If this turn configuration is maintained a series of spiral turns will ensue, causing a severe and rapid loss of altitude.

Half-brake turns   These are initiated from the half-brake position and may be either depression turns (depress right toggle to turn right, for example) or elevation turns (raise left toggle to turn right). Depression turns give a faster response with minimal banking.

Full-brake turns   The canopy is barely maintaining flying speed, and by definition such turns must be elevation turns.

When turning the canopy always be aware of your altitude and always check your airspace in the direction to which you are turning. For safety reasons RAPS students on their initial descents should never turn the canopy below 500ft. With experience this height may be reduced to 200ft.

Airspeed versus groundspeed   Each type of canopy has its own performance characteristics. **Airspeed** is the inherent forward speed of the canopy and is determined by several factors: weight of the jumper, angle of incidence (trim), aspect ratio and wing section among them. This airspeed is constant for any given brake setting.

Groundspeed is the resultant of airspeed plus or minus windspeed, depending on the direction in which the canopy is facing. It is most critical during the landing approach and touchdown. It is axiomatic that all ram-air canopies be landed into wind to minimise groundspeed. Figure 2.6 illustrates this principle.

Flight drills

From an open canopy height of 3,000ft, time in the air is approximately three minutes. The descent may appropriately be divided into three distinct phases, namely:

Safety checks
Effects of controls
Approach and landing

Essential actions   Before considering each phase in detail, let us examine the essential actions carried out by every jumper on every descent. These are carried out in strict order of priority as under. On deployment:

LOOK UP	Check canopy
RELEASE BRAKES	
ENSURE SLIDER DOWN	Pump brakes if necessary
LOOK AROUND	For other jumpers—steer away if necessary
LOCATE DROP ZONE	
STEER FOR DROP ZONE	
FACE INTO WIND NO	
LOWER THAN 500ft	(Student jumper)

If, on your first jump, you do no more than this you will have made a successful descent. In the three minutes flying time available, however, you can

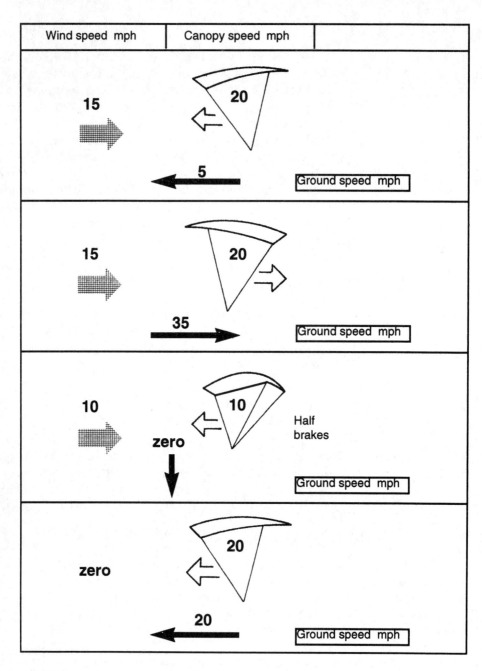

Figure 2.6
Canopy airspeed
and canopy
groundspeed

achieve more than this, so be positive, fly the canopy, and always try to get the most training value from every descent.

Safety checks   Check the canopy thoroughly, make sure it is flying correctly, that the end cells are properly inflated and that the slider is fully down. If the slider remains stuck higher up the lines, pump hard on the brakes until it comes down.

As you are doing this, check your airspace ahead and behind, above and below for other jumpers and take avoiding action if required. Remember the lower jumper has right of way.

Your next potential hazard is an out landing; make sure you know where you are in relation to the ideal opening point and the Drop Zone, and orientate your canopy accordingly. For your own safety you must make sure you land on the drop zone even at the expense of missing out any canopy handling exercises you may have been briefed to do.

Effects of controls   The following sequence is suggested for the first few jumps.

Now you have a good canopy, have your own airspace and are happy with your position in relation to the DZ, check your height and carry out the following handling exercises:

FACE THE DZ AND APPLY FULL BRAKE PROGRESSIVELY AND SMOOTHLY.

Note the change in slider noise and the way the canopy reacts. Release the brakes in the same manner.

CHECK HEIGHT AND POSITION IN RELATION TO THE DZ, THEN MAKE A FULL GLIDE TURN.

Check your airspace is clear, then hold one toggle down until you have turned through 360 degrees. On a student canopy this should take about 10 seconds. If you judge you then have time, turn the canopy through 360 degrees in the opposite direction.

NOW YOU KNOW HOW THE CANOPY TURNS AND HOW IT REACTS TO BRAKES

Holding Pattern Your next move is to fly the canopy on half brakes and assess your drift. From about 2,000ft, set up a holding pattern outside the target area. Apply half brakes and fly the canopy in a series of long S turns or zig-zags facing the target area. This will cause you to lose height without gaining too much distance. It will also accustom you to handling the canopy on half brakes—a useful configuration as it gives you a reserve of speed and a reserve of brakes. Keep your eye on the target, watch your height, and decide where you are going to start your downwind leg.

Approach and landing (Figure 2.7)

DOWNWIND LEG
From about 1500ft, fly the parachute on the downwind leg on half brakes, approximately 300 metres to one side of the target.

CROSSWIND (BASE) LEG
At about 1,000ft turn 90 degrees on to your crosswind (or base) leg. The point at which you make this turn

Figure 2.7
Target approach and landing pattern

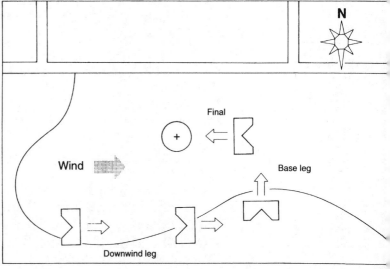

will be considered in more detail in Chapter 5 (**Basic Accuracy**) but for the moment remember that in high wind conditions (that is, of 15mph or over) you should make this turn no more than 50 metres past the target.

FINALS

At a height no lower than 500ft, turn the canopy through 90 degrees once more directly into the surface wind. Maintain half brakes.

At a height of about 100ft (minimum) let up on both toggles and fly the canopy at maximum airspeed toward the target.

At 10–15 feet above the ground, apply full brake smoothly, hold the brakes down and step on to the ground (See Lesson 4, **Parachute Landings**).

Some additional points

Carrying out these exercises as briefed presupposes the jumpmaster has given you a reasonable spot. Remember your safety brief—locate DZ and steer for DZ. Your first job is to make certain you land in a safe area. In order to ensure this, you must be aware of three additional techniques. These are: **running, holding, and crabbing** (Figure 2.8).

Figure 2.8
Canopy control: running; holding crabbing

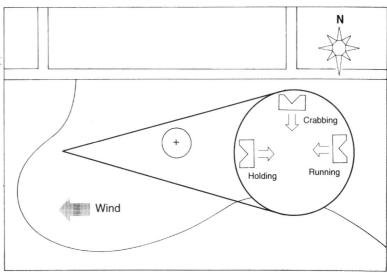

Running All this means is keeping the toggles high and letting the canopy run on full drive with the wind in order to gain maximum distance if you have been dropped too far away. Keep an eye on the target and on your altimeter, also on any potential obstacles on the ground. Once you are within striking distance of the DZ, come back to half brakes and remember you **must** turn into wind by 500ft.

Holding This is the converse of running, and is the technique to adopt if you have been dropped too close, particularly in strong upper winds (winds above 1,000ft). Face the canopy into the wind on full drive and check your position relative to the target. Check your height and check especially that you are not going to back into any obstacles outside the DZ. If this seems likely, make up your mind early and turn and run to clear them.

Crabbing This entails turning the canopy at 90 degrees to the wind line on full drive in order to get back on the wind line. Once you are positioned correctly in relation to the target, go back on to half brakes and carry on.

Summary of flight drills

Exit 3,000ft	SAFETY COUNT 1000, 2000, 3000, 4000,
	CHECK CANOPY
	BRAKES OFF
	SLIDER DOWN
	LOOK AROUND
2,700ft	FULL BRAKES AND RECOVER
2,500ft	360 DEGREE RIGHT AND LEFT TURNS
2,000ft	HALF BRAKES ZIGZAG IN HOLDING PATTERN
1,500ft	HALF BRAKES DOWNWIND
1,000ft	CROSSWIND (BASE) LEG
500ft	FINALS
100ft	FULL DRIVE
10–15ft	FLARE!!

This sequence is recommended for the first few descents and may be modified in the light of experience. Combine these techniques and try to learn from each jump. It is always a good idea to start thinking accuracy from about the 1500ft mark, although with experience after a few jumps the 1,000ft/500ft box pattern can be shortened. Never forget also to keep a constant lookout for other jumpers. Always aim to land on the target, after all, you have to land somewhere, so why not in the middle? (**but not at the expense of a safe landing**). See Chapter 5 (**Basic Accuracy**) for a follow-up to this section.

The wind drift indicator (WDI) (Section 8.2.e).

The WDI is a strip of crepe paper 22 feet × 10 inches, normally coloured red and yellow to ensure visibility from the air and weighted so as to give it a descent rate of about 20fps, which is the same rate of descent as an average-weight jumper under an unmodified canopy (see Glossary). At the start of each programme the WDI is dropped by the jumpmaster on the first load at a height of 2,000ft directly above the target.

The WDI drifts downwind and its position is noted by the JM and pilot and a prominent feature on the ground equidistant upwind is plotted. This is the opening point. The line from the opening point through the target to the WDI is known as the Wind Line (Figure 2.9). Once the load has jumped, these details are chinagraphed on the airphoto of the Drop Zone at the Manifest Area for the benefit of all jumpers who may not have observed the WDI.

If conditions are seen to be changing, another WDI may be thrown at any time either to validate the opening point or to establish a new one. If jumping has been suspended for any reason for a period exceeding 30 minutes, another WDI must be dropped in any case.

As the RAPS student will be under a full canopy at about 3,000ft, this opening point could well be extended (deeper) to allow for the extra time in the air and the (possibly) stronger winds at that height. The

Figure 2.9 The wind drift indicator

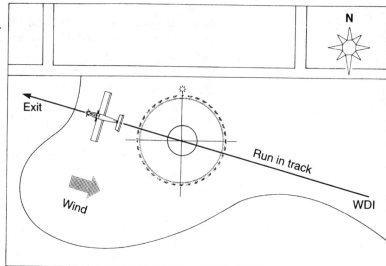

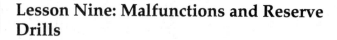

function of the WDI will be considered in more detail in Chapter 6 **(Spotting)**.

Lesson Nine: Malfunctions and Reserve Drills

Introduction: the reserve parachute

The reserve parachute in a RAPS assembly may be either a steerable round canopy, or may be another ram-air canopy; both types will be discussed below. For the static line student, however, the principal difference between the main and the reserve is that whereas the former is opened automatically by the static line, the reserve parachute must be opened manually by the jumper. There are three methods of opening the reserve:

1. By pulling the reserve handle
2. Indirectly through the reserve static line (RSL) once the main is cut away
3. By operation of the Automatic Activation Device (AAD) if the preset height and speed parameters are breached.

Which of these three methods comes into play depends on the circumstances of the main parachute failure and all three will be examined below.

Deployment sequence   Once the pin is pulled a spring-loaded pilot chute is released into the airflow. This pilot chute then exerts drag which initiates the opening sequence. Round reserve canopies normally have the suspension lines stowed in a diaper (see Glossary) which ensures a line-first deployment and thus reduces opening shock.

The round reserve parachute   This reserve parachute is typically aeroconical in shape with a flying diameter of 16ft, a descent rate between 18 and 22fps and a forward speed of 5–8mph. The forward speed of the canopy is the result of excess air pressure inside the canopy being expelled through the drive slots at the rear. The aeroconical shape and the drive slots give stability so that oscillation is virtually eliminated. Deployment is by means of a spring-loaded extractor parachute.

The ram-air reserve parachute   For reasons of bulk, it would be impractical in a sport assembly to have a ram-air reserve the same size as the main; ram-air reserve parachutes are conventionally smaller and less bulky. Nevertheless, in a student assembly, care must be taken to ensure that the reserve is sufficiently docile to be handled safely by an inexperienced jumper. A square reserve is deployed by means of a spring-loaded extractor parachute and free bag (see Glossary).

Malfunctions of the main parachute

Malfunctions occur for various reasons. Incorrect packing is one cause. A poor body position during the deployment sequence can also cause a parachute to malfunction. Equipment failure is another—though rarer—cause. From the above we can see that attention to detail in packing, correct training and progression, and good maintenance and inspection of equipment can go a long way towards eliminating parachute malfunctions.

Parachute malfunctions fall broadly into two classes: **total** and **partial**. These classifications are defined below, but it is emphasised that a partial malfunction does not necessarily denote a less urgent problem.

Total malfunctions—static line and freefall   A total malfunction occurs when the main container, for whatever reason, fails to open at all.

In static-line jumping, this would occur if the jumper were not hooked up or if the static line were to break.

In a freefall situation, a total malfunction would happen if the cable release were to jam or if the jumper was unable for any reason to locate or operate the release or hand-deploy.

If you have a total malfunction, pull your reserve immediately, regardless of body attitude.

Partial malfunctions—static line and freefall   A partial malfunction means that the canopy is out of the container, but has not opened fully/correctly. The most common type of partial malfunction is the **line over**, in which some part of the canopy has deployed through the lines (Figure 2.10). The canopy will almost certainly be rotating and the rate of descent will be excessive.

A second type of partial malfunction is the **streamer**. This is a high speed partial malfunction and occurs when the canopy fails to inflate at all, usually because the slider becomes jammed at the top of the lines (Figure 2.11).

Thirdly, there may be **canopy damage**, although this is rare in isolation.

Figure 2.10 A lineover malfunction

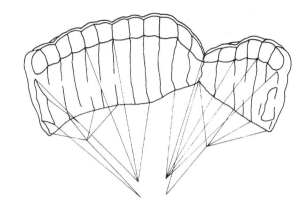

Figure 2.11 A streaming malfunction

Partial malfunctions—freefall only A **bag lock** means that the lines are fully extended but the canopy for some reason remains in the bag (Figure 2.12).

In any of the above situations, the main canopy must be cut away and the reserve pulled immediately.

The reason for cutting away the main canopy is to ensure there is no chance of the reserve pilot chute becoming entangled with the malfunctioned main. It

Figure 2.12 A bag lock

will be realised that, with the reserve static line (RSL) being a compulsory feature of student RAPS equipment, the very act of cutting away will result in the reserve being opened. However this may be, **you** have cut away and **you** must follow through by pulling the reserve handle even though the RSL will undoubtedly beat you to it.

Other malfunctions Two other types of malfunction will here be considered separately. They are a **horseshoe malfunction** and **pilot chute in tow**. In the UK, the bag-deployed static line method is universal so these two can only occur on a freefall descent.

A horseshoe malfunction occurs when the pilot chute snags on some part of the jumper's body and the rest of the canopy and lines come out above his head. This can also occur with a throwaway pilot chute which remains in its pocket when the bridle is accidentally snagged, thus releasing the pin and opening the container.

A horseshoe malfunction should be dealt with initially by trying to clear the snagging. If this does not clear immediately, **cut away and pull the reserve**.

A pilot chute in tow occurs when the bridle line extends but for some reason the bag fails to lift. In the case of a pilot chute in tow, **pull your reserve immediately**.

Malfunctions are a fact of parachuting life but they can be minimised by taking a responsible attitude to your jumping. Maintain your gear correctly and pack conscientiously. Stick to your briefed progression. Stick to your briefed opening height. Above all, **stay alert**.

Reserve drills

For the sake of simplicity and standardisation many CCIs teach a unified reserve drill which is designed to cope with all malfunctions, total and partial. This reserve drill involves cutting away the main canopy by operating the cutaway pad with the right hand, then pulling the reserve parachute with the left. This drill is summarised as follows:

LOOK	at cutaway pad and reserve handle
LOCATE	right hand on cutaway pad, left hand on reserve handle, with left thumb inside the handle
PEEL	velcro on cutaway pad from the bottom upwards
PUNCH	cutaway pad downwards to full arms length with RIGHT HAND—thus cutting away the main canopy
PULL	reserve handle with LEFT HAND by extending left arm to full arms length

It is important, first, to LOOK at the cutaway pad and reserve handle, to ensure that both hands are correctly positioned, that is: LOCATED.

In order to ensure that both risers disconnect simultaneously, it is then important to grasp the cutaway pad in the right hand and to PEEL the velcro away from the bottom upwards before the PUNCH which disconnects the main canopy.

Finally ONCE THIS HAS BEEN DONE, it is important to

extend the left arm fully in order to pull the reserve handle cleanly in line with the cable housing.

There remains a division of opinion among experienced jumpers regarding the necessity of cutting away from a total malfunction. The educated jumper will be capable of formulating his own judgement as he progresses and will thus be able to handle each situation as and when it arises. As a student, however, it is essential that you learn, understand, and practise your reserve drills however they are taught.

The automatic activation device (AAD)

The FXC 12000   The manufacturer's instructions state that this must be pre-set on the ground prior to emplaning and that the main canopy opening must be at least 1500 feet above the unit preset release height. Thus, given the RAPS opening height of 3,000ft, the FXC would typically be set to a release height of 1500ft AGL. The FXC will then operate at a height of 1500ft if, and only if, the rate-of-descent sensor indicates a vertical speed in excess of 40fps.

The following operational conditions apply:

1. The FXC **will not operate** when the jumper is above the unit's height setting, regardless of his rate of descent.
2. The FXC **will not operate** when the jumper reaches the unit's height setting and his rate of descent is less than 40fps.
3. The FXC **will operate** when the jumper reaches the unit's height setting and his rate of descent exceeds 40fps.
4. The FXC **will operate** if the jumper is at or below the unit's height setting and his rate of descent changes from less than 40 to more than 40fps. It follows from the above that if the sortie is aborted for any reason and the aircraft descends with the jumpers still on board, the FXCs must be switched off to avoid firing in the aircraft.

The CYPRES CYPRES was designed specifically for the experienced jumper; there is, however, a student version available with wider operating parameters. CYPRES uses advanced electronics to sense pressure changes and the student version will operate when descent rate exceeds 43fps below 1,000ft altitude. Both experienced and student models will operate when descent rate exceeds 115fps at or below 750ft altitude. Once switched on, CYPRES will work for 14 hours before switching itself off. CYPRES can also be programmed to operate when jumping at a DZ of higher/lower elevation than the mounting airfield. CYPRES must be returned to the manufacturer every two years for servicing. The address can be found in the Glossary to this Manual.

Finally it must be re-emphasised here that the AAD is installed as a backup system to open the reserve. If you have a parachute malfunction, it is your responsibility to take the appropriate action and get your reserve flying.

Unusual ram-air deployments

The following unusual deployments do not necessarily require cutaway action and reserve activation:

Pilot chute hesitation (freefall only)
Closed end cells
Slider not completely down, canopy fully open
Premature brake release
Broken steering line
Broken suspension line
Line twists

These are merely nuisance factors which can normally be rectified as under:

Pilot chute hesitation: If this occurs it is usually on sub-terminal delays when the spring-loaded pilot chute does not clear the zone of depression created behind the jumper in a good arched position. You can remedy this by twisting the body and looking, thus causing the burble to break up. Keep the safety count going and be aware of the loss of altitude.

Closed end cells: It occasionally happens that the end cells fail to pressurise fully. Rectify by pumping hard on both brakes until the cells re-inflate.

Slider not completely down: The correct position for the slider is just above the connector links. Sometimes it may stick four or five feet higher up the lines. Rectify by pumping hard on both brakes.

Premature brake release: Normally caused by careless packing. The canopy will open with one brake set (half brake) and the other brake off (prematurely released during deployment). The canopy will thus be turning in the direction of the applied (half) brake. Confirm that this is what has happened, then simply release the other brake.

Broken steering line: The canopy will have to be steered on the rear risers. (Right riser to steer right, left to steer left). Be aware of heavier control forces. Do not attempt to control the canopy on the front risers.

Broken suspension line: Not on its own a sufficient reason to use the reserve. Along with the broken steering line, this problem should normally be avoided by correct inspection and maintenance.

Line twists: Mainly caused by rotation of the bag in the slipstream (static-line). Can be caused by unstable exit or unstable pull. Always look past the twists to check the canopy is fully deployed. Reach high on the risers and using the legs as a long lever, kick hard in the opposite direction until the twists come out. As the last twist comes out, force the risers apart to prevent the inertia putting twists in the direction you have been kicking.

These lessons conclude your basic course and you are now BPA Category One.

Briefings

Following your basic course, the next instruction you will be given will be a specific briefing for your first descent. Ideally, the first jump will be made on the second day of the course although sometimes this has to be postponed through adverse weather conditions. Your training record is in date typically for a period of two months from completion date of training or from the last descent. At our own Centre, if the time lapse exceeds two months, the following conditions apply:

2–6 months	Refresher training required
6–12 months	Retrain required
Over 12 months	Full re-course required

Most Centres will operate a similar system.

Physical fitness

Remember that parachute jumping is primarily a physical skill, so the emphasis throughout your course will have been on practising or simulating the associated activities and drills. Physical fitness is, of course, specific to the type of activity engaged in but your most successful jumper will certainly be well co-ordinated and reasonably agile. Stamina is also important, as even in the early stages you may be making three jumps per day and packing after each one. Parachuting uses up a lot of nervous energy and instruction can be better absorbed and skills more readily developed if the jumper is physically strong and mentally alert. The student who is serious about remaining in the sport should definitely embark upon some physical training programme if he is not already in one.

Your progression from now on will be via a graduated series of parachute jumps, each fully briefed, observed, and de-briefed. This progression will be examined in the next two chapters.

ENJOY YOUR FIRST JUMP

3

The Training Progression Part One: Categories 2-8

The Training Philosophy

The BPA Category system was originally based on the French syllabus of freefall progression and was introduced to this country in the early 1960s. It has since been modified and adapted to British requirements over the years by the Safety and Training Committee. The aim of the system is to provide a foundation of freefall skills through a series of progressive exercises which will enable you to jump with confidence and safety both alone and with others. The number of jumps at each height is the minimum considered necessary to ensure that each particular skill has been mastered. Another important principle is that you are given sufficient altitude to perform a particular exercise with safety at a realistic tempo. The workload is thus geared to the time available for its completion. All jumps will be observed and critiqued by the instructor. Progression through the system to Category 8 can be broadly divided into two phases: Categories 2–6, and Categories 7 and 8.

Categories 2–6 (static-line to 15 second delay. Opening height 3,000ft)

On your initial jumps the canopy will be static-line deployed. This is for safety reasons in order to ensure that you have mastered the basics of the exit and can demonstrate stability while performing dummy ripcord pulls (DRCPs) before moving on to freefall.

You will then progress to short delays of 5 and 10

seconds, counting throughout; for these jumps stability is maintained by the presentation of a symmetrical curved surface to the airflow (the ARCH). Once you have gained confidence in the air you can begin to relax this position, learn control, and attempt elementary manoeuvres. This confidence is developed by the successful completion of your 5 and 10 second delays and the continued propensity of the main parachute to open when you pull the handle.

Having demonstrated the ability to maintain aircraft heading for ten seconds, counting throughout, you are ready to progress to 15 second delays from a height of 5,000ft. Stability is now maintained in a more relaxed position and the emphasis is on longitudinal trim and automatic correction of any involuntary movement.

Categories 7 and 8 (20 to 35 second delay. 6,000–8,000ft. Opening height 3,000ft)

It is during this second phase, when you have learned to fall vertically (that is, without any forward movement and without backsliding) in the more relaxed box position introduced at Cat 6, that you are taught control in the form of turns and loops. Your confidence is given a big boost when you restabilize from a deliberately-induced tumble (unstable exit).

At the final stage you will be taught how to generate sufficient lift by body position to enable you to make horizontal distance (track). As your jump numbers build up, you will develop an increased awareness of elapsed time in freefall and will also improve your canopy handling skills.

The rate of progression

The category system only lays down a minimum number of jumps at each height. The rate of progression depends on a number of factors, continuity probably being one of the most significant, whatever stage you have reached. Twenty jumps made in a week will be far more beneficial than the same number carried out over a two-month period. It is the instructor's responsibility to observe each descent, analyse and correct faults and decide when, subject to the constraints of the system, progression to the next stage is appropriate.

A realistic objective must be given to each exercise and sufficient time allowed for its completion. Too little time will lead to the exercise being rushed whereas too much time will lead to a false sense of the tempo required. A certain amount of pressure is necessary to provide stimulus for action.

Requirements for each Category (Section 2.4).

Note: Exit heights throughout these briefings are given in relation to the RAPS opening height of 3,000ft AGL.

Category 1: Has received a minimum of six hours ground training and has been cleared to make a first static line descent.

Aim: Physical and mental preparation for the first jump.

Category 2: Has demonstrated the ability to fall in a stable position, counting throughout.

Descents: A minimum of two static-line jumps from a height of 3,000ft

Aim: Good exit, good stable position, good count

Coaching points: In the early stages, your exit must be forceful; you must go out **hard**. From a side door, angle the leading shoulder forwards to avoid turning outwards on exit. Remember that on exit, the airflow is horizontal so your position will be head-high. (Figure 3.1). Aim to achieve a symmetrical position with maximum arch immediately. Watch the jumpmaster and shout out the count. These jumps are designed to teach

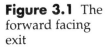

Figure 3.1 The forward facing exit

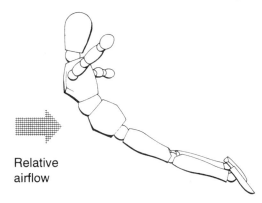

Relative
airflow

you the exit technique, which has to be mastered before we can move on. Two consecutive good ones required.

You will be taught to pack your own parachute under supervision at this stage (Section 6.8).

You are now ready to progress to dummy ripcord pulls in preparation for your first freefall

Category 3: Has demonstrated the ability to perform successful Dummy Ripcord Pulls (DRCPs), counting throughout, on three consecutive descents.

Descents: A minimum of three static line jumps from a height of 3,000ft.

Aim: Good exit, stable position maintained, co-ordinated arm movement, handle pulled, good recovery.

Coaching points: The first priority must be a good exit; do not attempt to rush the pull at the expense of a good position outside the door. Before you go for the handle, you **must** be established in a stable position on the airflow. Go for maximum arch with legs wide for lateral stability. So long as you maintain a hard arched position any hand and arm movements will not adversely affect stability. This one needs a lot of practice on the ground.

Progression to freefall will only take place after a minimum of five static line descents and will only be

authorised by an approved or advanced instructor.
The first freefall will take place no later than the day
following the last of the three successful DRCP
descents.

Category 4: Has demonstrated the ability to perform two consecutive delayed openings, counting throughout, of between three and five seconds.

Descents: A minimum of two freefall jumps from a
height of 3,500ft.

Aim: Good exit, stable position throughout, good
count, good stable pull.

Coaching points: Uppermost of course, is the psychological barrier of the first freefall. As a confidence booster, you should first pull the handle on the ground in training to be aware of the exact pull force required. Priority must be given to making a correct exit with the emphasis on maximum arch.

As you leave the door, concentrate on looking at the jumpmaster. This will give you a good point of reference. Remember your safety count after the pull; you will be briefed on the possibility of a pilot chute hesitation and the appropriate remedial action. Most CCIs give a three second delay on the first freefall so that the DRCP actions can be duplicated. Nevertheless, you should remember you have plenty of height; you will have to demonstrate a good 5 second delay with a good pull before being allowed to progress to 10 seconds.

Category 5: Has demonstrated the ability to perform two consecutive delayed openings of ten seconds, maintaining a heading and counting throughout.

Descents: A minimum of two freefall jumps from a
height of 4,200ft.

Aim: Good exit, stable position throughout, heading
maintained throughout, good stable pull on ten seconds.

Coaching points: The exit **must** have been mastered at this stage—no peeling off. The heading with the aircraft must be maintained, as the tendency to turn often results from a poor exit. This tendency may be corrected by gently leaning back onto aircraft heading. Watch the aircraft as you go away, then be aware of change of body attitude to a more horizontal position. Be aware of increased speed, arch hard and maintain symmetry. Concentrate on the ARCH as you pull. The pull must be perfect on 10 seconds, and this can be practised on the ground against a stopwatch.

Category 6: Has demonstrated the ability to perform two consecutive delayed openings of fifteen seconds, maintaining a heading. Has also demonstrated the ability to use an altimeter in freefall.

Descents: A minimum of two freefall jumps from a height of 5,000ft.

Aim: The jumper must now be able to fall vertically on heading in a relaxed box position for 15 seconds. Once this has been achieved, must be able to observe his altimeter in freefall and pull at the briefed height.

Horizontal trim: This involves awareness of body position to ensure that you are falling absolutely vertically, a factor that becomes increasingly important when you begin working with other jumpers at Cat 9.

To recap on the basic stable position: when the legs are fully extended it is important that the arms are spread with the hands at shoulder level. This symmetrical position will ensure you are falling flat, with no forward movement and no backsliding (Figure 3.2).

In order to maintain this trim in a more relaxed position it is necessary to reduce lift equally both forward of and behind the centre of gravity. Thus, if the legs are bent up there will be more lift at the top end and backsliding will result. Conversely, if the arms are bent

Figure 3.2 The basic spread position

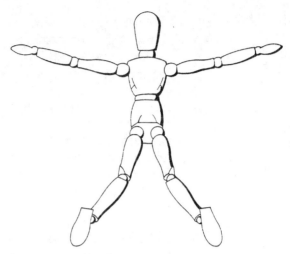

at the elbow and the legs remain long, forward movement will be induced.

The way to achieve a flat trim, therefore, from your wide stable spread position, is to bend up the legs and drop the elbows slightly. This will ensure that the hands remain at the level of the shoulders and longitudinal trim is maintained. This is known as the neutral box position and will be your basic working position from now on (Figure 3.3).

Because the effective surface area of the body has been reduced, the rate of descent will increase slightly and the effect of any control movement will be enhanced.

Figure 3.3 The box position

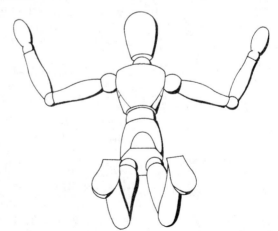

Coaching points: Good exit essential—go out in a wide position and maintain aircraft heading. After about 5 seconds, drop the elbows slightly and bend the legs by up to 60 degrees. Research your horizontal trim and maintain the count. Terminal velocity is reached after approximately 12 seconds. Heading must be maintained and involuntary turns corrected. Watch for asymmetrical positioning of arms and legs. Stability is now maintained not by a hard arch but in a flatter position with the legs bent upwards and heading is maintained by feeling the airflow and by compensatory body/limb movements as needed. Keep the count going—15 seconds. This must also be practised on the ground against the stopwatch.

Buffeting, which is an irregular longitudinal oscillation, may be caused if the arms or legs are out of trim, or if the body remains arched. Correct by flattening the body and checking the positioning of arms and legs.

There should be no progression beyond 15 seconds until this new position has been mastered

Reading the altimeter

The altimeter may be either wrist- or chest- mounted. To observe it in freefall in either instance the following procedure should be carried out: from your relaxed box position, stretch the arms slightly forward and drop the chin slightly to observe the chest altimeter; if it is wrist-mounted, this forward movement of the arms will also bring it into your field of vision. Remember the height loss during the deployment sequence—if you pull at 3,200ft indicated, your canopy will be open at about 3,000ft.

A general word about altimeters: remember they are delicate precision instruments and should not be subject to rough usage. They are set to zero on the flight line before the jump; if the DZ is at a different location from the mounting airfield and consequently at a different field elevation then allowance for this height differential must be made. Thus if the DZ is 500ft

higher than the mounting airfield, the altimeter should be set **back to minus 500ft.** The altimeter should be checked during the ride to altitude with the on-board master altimeter.

You are now ready to learn turns

Category 7: Has demonstrated the ability to perform controlled 360 degree turns in both directions.

Descents: No minimum descent requirement. Normally needs at least three descents from 6,000ft (20 second delays).

Aim: To be able to turn accurately in both directions.

Principles of turning: Turning the body in a horizontal plane involves a controlled loss of symmetry. In order to turn, the propeller principle is employed in that the upper body and arms are angled in such a way as to cause air deflection which initiates and maintains the turn (Figure 3.4).

The speed of the rotation is dependent on the following:

1. The amount of air pressure (falling speed)
2. The length of the moment arm
3. The angle of the turning surface to the airflow

Coaching points: Should tighten up position slightly. Can make one consolidation descent if required, that is, a 20 second delay in tighter position, pulling on altimeter at 3,000ft.

Exercise 1—360 degree left turn.
Fallaway and reduce position for 10 seconds. Select heading; look left then rotate upper body and arms as one unit downwards (about 15–20 degrees) to the left. Angle the hands also. Stop turn by opposite counter movement then adopt neutral position as heading comes up. Keep mental count going and pull on altimeter at 3,000ft .

Figure 3.4
Initiation of a left
turn

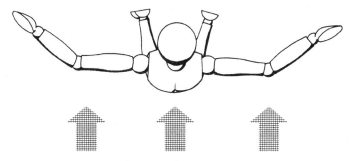

Relative airflow

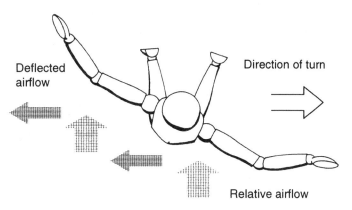

Exercise 2—360 degree right turn.
As above, look and rotate to the right.

Exercise 3—360 degree left and right turns.
As above; fallaway 10 seconds, turn 360 degrees left, as
the heading comes up counter and initiate turn to the
right. Stop the turn on heading; keep your mental
count going and pull on altimeter at 3,000ft.

These exercises may require more than one jump each.
Students should not be progressed until alternate 360
degree turns can be performed accurately and under
control as the ability to turn naturally is the basis for all
future learning.

**You have now learned to turn in alternate directions
with precision and are ready to progress to Category
8 exercises from a height of 8,000ft (35 second delays)**

Category 8: Has demonstrated the ability to perform the following:

(a) An unstable exit
(b) A dive exit
(c) Back loops
(d) Tracks, including a track turn as an avoidance manoeuvre
(e) A backloop, 360 degree left turn, 360 degree right turn, a short track and waveoff, from a minimum altitude of 8,000ft.

NB 1. No tracking exercises may be commenced below an exit altitude of 7,000ft AGL.

2. Category 8 parachutists and above may use 'throwaway' pilot chutes.

3. Conversion jumps to 'throwaway' pilot chute for parachutists below 'C' certificate must be made on equipment fitted with an AAD.

4. All briefs for equipment conversions, up to 'C' certificate must be given by an Instructor.

Descents: No minimum descent requirement. Exercises normally carried out from a height of 8,000ft (35 second delays).

Unstable exit This is designed as a confidence builder, and to demonstrate your ability to recover from the instability which will inevitably occur at some stage as you practise subsequent Cat 8 exercises. Leave the aircraft in a crouched position, grab the knees and pull them hard to the chest. This will result in a tumbling fallaway which may or may not be rotating. Hold for three or four seconds, then arch hard. The tumbling will immediately stop and you will be falling face to earth. Locate a heading, tighten up your position and use the rest of the descent to consolidate your turning ability. Keep the mental count going and pull on altimeter at 3,000ft.

Dive exit (Figure 3.5) All previous exits have been made facing the airflow; now we have to learn to make a stable dive facing the other way. This method of leaving the aircraft is most commonly used in Formation Skydiving (FS) exercises where a fast exit is totally essential to stay within working distance of the other jumper(s). We have already discovered that our position on the relative wind after exit has been head high and legs low (Figure 3.1). If we are now to reverse this position we will find the legs very high and the head very low. If we fail to counteract this tendency we will certainly go very head-down and will probably execute a forward loop.

In order to avoid too steep an angle, lift must be increased at the top of the body and almost totally reduced at the legs. Therefore the arms must be extended forward as far as possible and the head kept back. The legs must immediately be tucked up against the backside. In addition, the dive must be made facing directly aft. Position yourself at the forward edge of the door, kneeling on the inside knee with the sole of the outside foot braced against the door frame and push off straight towards the tail of the aircraft. If the dive is made outwards at an angle to the airflow, rolling or other instability may be induced. The emphasis on this exit should be on neatness—arms well forward and no more than shoulder-width apart, head well back and legs tucked up hard. This will enable you to maintain eye contact with the previous jumper and to stay with him. For the rest of the descent you should concentrate on consolidating turns. Remember, too, that you are still in the throw-forward for about 10 seconds, this time facing aft. The resulting body angle will affect your performance if you attempt other manoeuvres too early.

Backloops (Figure 3.6) The forces producing a successful backloop are both dynamic and aerodynamic. To achieve a good backloop, the following procedure should be followed: leave the aircraft in an orthodox forward-facing exit; fallaway for ten seconds reducing into your box position and picking up a heading. Then extend the arms forward at shoulder width and beat down with the hands just brushing the thighs.

Figure 3.5 The
dive exit

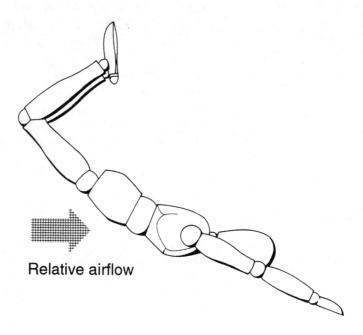

Relative airflow

Simultaneously lift the knees toward the chest and
throw the head back—**dynamic action**. The lift given
by the arms going forward and the bent legs going up
will cause the body to rise and start to rotate backwards—**aerodynamic action**. Unless immediate action
is taken to stop this rotation it will continue. Once the
arms have reached the limit of the backward extension, the palms should be reversed and the arms swept
forwards. This restores lift to the leg area before the
jumper starts to ride up and prevents a second loop.
This braking action is reinforced by extending the legs
then arching hard. This manoeuvre is all about timing.
A backloop will take about one second to execute so all
arm and body movements must be fully co-ordinated.
Initiation must be dynamic and positive, as must the
recovery. The arms should be extended forward at

Figure 3.6 The backloop

1. Extend arms, head back, knees to chest

2. Aerodynamic lift, start of rotation

3. Rotation onto the back, arms remain horizontal

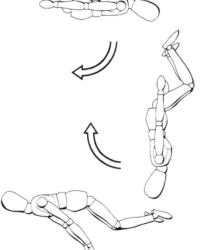

4. Rotating through the vertical

5. Braking the rotation, action of arms plus leg extension

6. Arch hard

shoulder width, if wider they are more likely to be asymmetrical, causing the jumper to roll off the top of the loop. The jumper should maintain altitude awareness and be in a stable position face to earth at no lower than 4,000ft. Better to achieve two or three good loops from 8,000ft than rush the exercise and achieve nothing.

Backloops should initially be practised as a specific exercise on one jump and not be combined with any other (eg dive exits) at this stage. It is much more effective to learn one skill at a time.

Tracking Tracking is the achievement of optimum horizontal movement in freefall, that is, the maximum forward speed combined with minimum height loss. It is an essential freefall skill with many applications, namely:

Formation Skydiving—moving back to and catching up with a formation; breakoff from a formation—all jumpers turn 180 degrees and track to achieve safe separation before opening

Demo jumping—normally with smoke to demonstrate horizontal movement to the public

Safety—to get back to the opening point and thus make the DZ after a bad spot

Naturally, the angle of descent, along with vertical and horizontal speeds can be adjusted according to the situation. In an aerofoil track the average horizontal distance gained is 10 per cent of the height loss; an optimum track position will give about 20 per cent, that is, 200ft of horizontal movement for every 1,000ft of altitude lost. From this it can be seen that in a max. track from 12,000ft about 500 yards at best can be covered. This is ignoring the effect of winds at altitude.

The minimum exit height for tracking is 7,000ft (Section 2.4 Cat 8). 8,000ft, giving a 35 second delay, is about right. Tracking is normally taught after backloops have been mastered and the following sequence is recommended:

Exercise 1 (Flat track)
Exit deep, facing forward on aircraft heading. Turn 180 degrees to face target; After 10 seconds, straighten the legs and point the toes; feet should be about 12 inches apart; simultaneously bring the arms down to full stretch with the palms down and about 6 inches out from and level with the thighs (Figure 3.7).

Figure 3.7 The flat track position

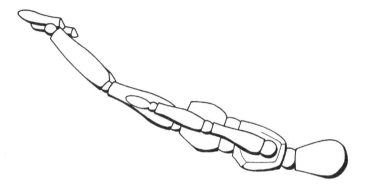

The body should be flat, that is, no arch and the head should be forced back. There should be maximum tension in the body to maintain a rigid position. The effect of the foregoing is to bring the body into a more head-down position at an angle of about 45 degrees to the horizontal; because of this alteration in angle there is an increase in vertical speed. The effect of the airflow working on the inclined body is to impart a horizontal force which enables the jumper to glide forwards. It is important to maintain a mental count and altitude awareness throughout the jump. If stability is lost, arch hard, check height and try again. After 30 seconds (from 8,000ft), sweep the arms forward and flare out into a normal stable position, check altimeter, and pull. **Don't** pull in the track. . . .
You may have to repeat Exercise 1 several times before you are confident in your ability to maintain stability and heading at this new angle. One common fault is fishtailing, a side to side movement caused by

loose legs. Another is buffeting, which will be induced if the body is arched. Remember, the more rigidly the body is held in a straight line, the more efficient will be this particular position. When you are confident in the flat track, you are ready to move into the track proper—the aerofoil track.

Exercise 2 (Aerofoil track)
Initiate as before, move into your flat track position and as you pick up speed bring the feet closer together, point the toes hard, force the head still further back, suck in the stomach and roll the shoulders forward. Flex the body slightly from the waist, cup the hands and push the arms downwards onto the airflow slightly below the line of the body. The total effect is a controlled de-arch which shapes the torso into an aerofoil section (Figure 3.8).

Figure 3.8 The aerofoil track position

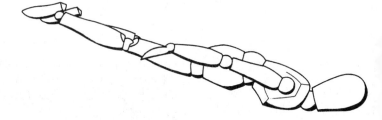

Because the legs are closer together and more lift is created at the top end of the body a flatter glide angle is achieved and stability is maintained despite the de-arch because of the increase in speed. The optimum glide angle should be researched by moving the arms by degrees onto the airflow. Too far below the bodyline will cause buffeting; the hands must not be allowed to act as airbrakes.

Exercise 3 (Track turns)
Initiate as before and move into the aerofoil track position. Turns are accomplished by slightly turning the head and leaning gently into the desired direction of turn. Because of the speed buildup, the turn will fol-

low a curved path; no attempt should be made to initiate an abrupt 180 degree turn. To facilitate telemeter observation hold the outward track for about 15 seconds at 90 degrees to aircraft heading, then you should lean back towards the DZ until the 180 degree turn is complete and come back to the opening point. Maintain altitude awareness at all times. The Cat. 8 requirement is for track turns as an avoidance manoeuvre; successful completion of the above exercise will have demonstrated your ability to make any degree of turn.

The Category 8 qualifying jump   This must be made from a minimum altitude of 8,000ft and consists of alternate 360 degree turns, a backloop, short track and waveoff. This qualifying jump should be aerially critiqued. As with all tests, it should be no problem at all, providing you have done the previous work correctly.

Leave the aircraft on heading, fallaway 10 seconds, pick up a heading, turn 360 degrees left, 360 degrees right; check, set yourself up for your backloop; loop, short track, check height, wave off at 3,5000ft and pull at 3,000ft.

Congratulations; you are now Category eight and ready to progress to Formation Skydiving through categories nine and ten.

The throwaway pilot chute

As a Category eight jumper, you are now qualified to convert to a throwaway, or hand-deployed, pilot chute. This pilot chute has no spring and is packed into a small Spandex pocket which may be positioned either on the legstrap or on the bottom of the main container (BOC).

Hand-deployed pilot chutes were introduced to the sport in about 1975 along with the general revolution in kit design inspired by the rapid development of Formation Skydiving in the United States. Working in close proximity to, and in contact with, other jumpers, posed the obvious risk of accidental snagging of the main ripcord handle which was conventionally positioned on the main harness on the right hand side level with the chest strap (outboard pull).

In order to counter this risk, the bridle line (see Glossary) was extended and the container was now closed by a curved pin stitched into the bridle. There was now no longer any need for the pilot chute to be spring-loaded as it was now to be positioned externally to the container. The pilot chute was packed into a small pocket and withdrawn by the jumper by means of a toggle. On being released into the airflow, the pilot chute extended the bridle, withdrew the pin which opened the container and then continued its normal function of applying drag to deploy the main canopy.

Any pilot chute, spring loaded or hand-deployed, must be allowed to function unimpeded. Hence the emphasis on always pulling in a stable position. With a throwaway, there exists the new possibility of the pilot chute snagging on the jumper's wrist or forearm unless the correct technique is applied.

The pilot chute must be withdrawn from the pocket in such a way that it **always remains behind the forearm**. The arm is then extended and the wrist turned (pronated) so that the pilot chute is released from the back of the hand. It must be released as soon as the arm is at full stretch. Do not hang on to the pilot chute because the drag on the bridle may pull the pin and open the container prematurely.

4

The Training Progression Part Two: Categories 9 and 10

The Training Philosophy

When you have reached Category 8, you can begin to learn the techniques of Formation Skydiving. Formation Skydiving is where one or more skydivers link together (holding hands) to build a formation. The name Formation Skydiving was given to this aspect of the Sport by the International Parachute Commission in 1992. This was done in anticipation of the sport becoming an Olympic event. Before 1992 Formation Skydiving was known as Relative Work. This was a more appropriate title because skydivers alter their body position to control their rate of descent and horizontal position to allow themselves to remain relative to each other. During the remainder of your progression training you will learn the techniques to enable you to fly relative to another skydiver or a formation. Through this phase of your progression the training is in two distinct parts, Category 9 and 10. During Category 9 you will practise the individual techniques of Formation Skydiving with the assistance of an instructor or coach.

During Category 10 you will combine the many skills you learned during your Category 9 training to build four formations with three other skydivers. After the successful completion of the Category 10 skydive you can look forward to jumping with other people at any level. Your progression will obviously be faster if you train with jumpers of a higher standard than yourself.

Category 9: Has been introduced to Formation Skydiving (FS) by CCI nominated Instructors or Category 10 jumpers of proven FS instructional ability, and has achieved either WARP Level 7, or has demonstrated the ability to:

(a) **Control fall rate**
(b) **Control horizontal movement (forwards, backwards and sideways)**
(c) **Achieve docking techniques**
(d) **Turn in place**
(e) **Dive and approach a target.**

Descents: There is no minimum number of descents. A student may progress when the instructor or coach is satisfied with ability level.

Aim: To develop good and safe individual flying skills.

Coaching points:

Body position   Many sports have a balanced stance that is commonly used as a set-up position for other moves. In Formation Skydiving your balanced stance will be the box position. The box is very important because it is your neutral flying position. In skydiving neutral means there is no horizontal movement. You will be falling straight down, what we call falling 'down the tube'. When you make your moves during a skydive you will leave the box position, however you must return to it once you have completed your move. The box position will require you to alter slightly the freefall position you will have become used to so far. The specific details of the box position are as follows:

– the head is up and looking forward
– the upper arms are at 90 degrees to the body
– the elbows are bent 90 degrees and the elbows are no further back than the level of the shoulders

- the knees are at least shoulder width apart
- the lower legs are extended slightly into the wind
- the body is slightly arched from knees to chest (Figure 4.1)

Figure 4.1 The neutral fall-rate position

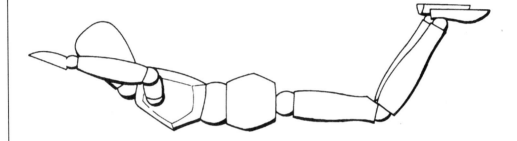

Fall rate control

You must be able to make minor alterations in your rate as you fall 'down the tube'. This is to allow you to compensate for the fall rate of other skydivers and for the changes in fall rate that can occur during a Formation Skydive. You can control your fall rate by using upward movement to slow your fall rate and downward movement to increase your fall rate.

Upward movement   You can achieve upward movement by decreasing the arch of your box position. This will allow you to make subtle changes to your fall rate. To do this you maintain the symmetry of your box position, but decrease the arch by raising the hips and pushing down with shoulders, elbows and knees (Figure 4.2).

Figure 4.2 The
slow fall-rate
position

Downward movement   You can achieve downward
movement by increasing the arch of your box position.
This will allow you to reduce vertical separation and
make subtle changes to your fall rate. To increase your
arch push your hips forward and pull your shoulders
and knees up (Figure 4.3).

Figure 4.3 The
fast fall-rate posi-
tion

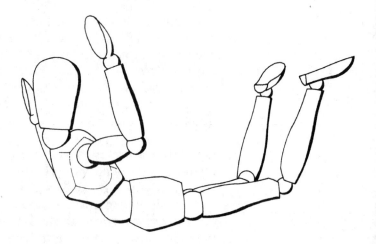

Control of horizontal movement

If you wish to be a successful skydiver you must be able to move in three directions. In addition to controlling your fall rate, you must be able to move in all directions in the horizontal plane, that is forwards, backwards and sideways. To produce horizontal movement, you must deflect air in the opposite direction to that you wish to travel. This deflection is produced by using the legs, arms and torso and will be explained in detail for each movement.

Forward movement You will have already experienced some forward movement when you carried out your tracking exercises. However, the forward movement we are looking for is controlled forward movement over distances of 10–15 feet. Forward movement is produced by deflecting the air with your lower legs; this will provide the force to move you forward.

The details of this movement are: the arms remain in the box position while your lower legs extend symmetrically into the slipstream until your knees are locked and your toes are pointed. Maintaining the knees shoulder width distance apart will keep your legs widespread which will increase your lateral stability and directional control (Figure 4.4).

Figure 4.4
Moving forward

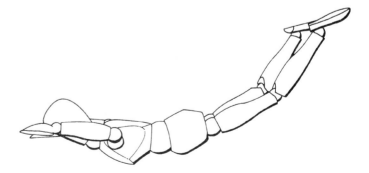

Backward movement Backward movement is achieved by deflecting air with the arms and upper body while increasing the airflow over the lower body. The details of this movement are: press down with the shoulders and elbows and push the hands forward and down. Simultaneously lift the thighs and the knees (Figure 4.5).

Figure 4.5
Moving backward

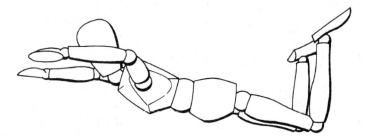

Sideways movement Sideways movement is achieved by using the body and legs to deflect air to the opposite side of the body. The details for moving the body sideways to the left are as follows: push down the left shoulder, elbow and the left-hand side of the torso. Press the left knee down and lay the lower legs over to the right. (Figure 4.6).

Docking techniques

The ability to join a formation, or as it is known 'dock' on a formation and flying in a formation is an important part of Formation Skydiving. This is true whether you are jumping with a 4-way group or taking part in a 250-way record attempt.

The essential part of docking on a formation is for you to arrive at your position or slot in the formation with little or no momentum. To do this, as you are moving forward and you reach approximately one body's length from your target, relax into your box position and you will have sufficient momentum to coast towards your slot.

Figure 4.6
Moving sideways

Having arrived in your slot you must now take the correct grips and fly the formation. The grips could be somebody's wrists, arms or legs. You take hold of the grips while maintaining your box position. Keep your elbows higher than your shoulders. Keeping your elbows high will prevent you from cupping air with your upper body and altering the fall rate of the formation. In addition, to help you fly the formation, extend the lower legs into the relative wind until you feel you could let go of the grips and remain in place. The extension of the legs, together with keeping your elbows high while holding the grips, will allow you to fly with the formation and not affect the formation's fall rate.

Turn in place

To turn in place you must turn round your body's centre point which will be just above your hips. To do this you must simultaneously deflect air with your upper and lower parts of your body in a similar air deflection position to that of a propeller. You will have already learned to turn by using the upper body during your category 1–8 training; you must now also use the lower body to give a centre point turn.

A good centre point turn starts with a good balanced box position. To turn to the right, lower your left knee and hip and lay your lower legs to the right, simultaneously bank the upper body to the right while lowering your right arm and shoulder (Figure 4.7). The symmetry of your box position must be maintained throughout the turn.

Figure 4.7 A centre point turn

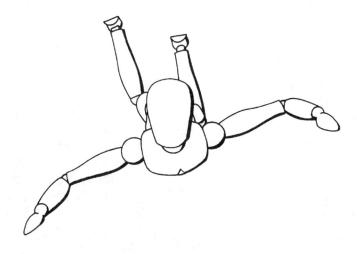

You should maintain eye contact for as long as possible with your partner or coach throughout your turn. To do this keep your head facing forward and maintain the eye contact using your peripheral vision.

Dive and approach to a target

To close long distances where you have vertical and horizontal separation (that is your target is below and in front of you) you must use diving techniques. The dive position is similar to the track position except the hands are 12 inches from the body and the upper body is arched. (Figure 4.8) This position will generate both forward and downward movement. The angle of the dive is controlled by the amount of upper body arch you apply. If you have a considerable amount of vertical and horizontal distance to cover, you must use a staged approach. Use the dive to close half the distance to your target then recover to your box position. Once you are back in your box position assess whether you can close the remaining distance by normal forward and downward movement or do you need to dive again. If you need to dive again, dive until you have closed half the remaining distance and then reassess. The aim is to reach a point where you are level with your target, at a distance of 6–12 feet out. You can then close that distance by simple forward movement.

Figure 4.8 The dive position

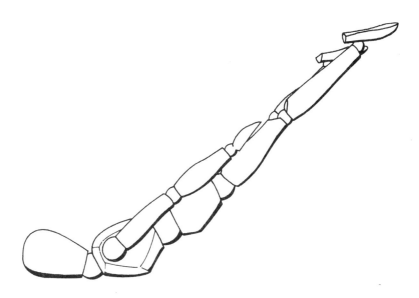

Category 10: Has achieved WARP level 10, or has demonstrated the ability to complete four points of 4-way Formation Skydiving.

NB 1. No Category 8 jumpers and no more than 2 Category 9 jumpers per group
    2. D Certificate parachutists and above may use pullout pilot chutes

Training criteria During this phase of your progression you will combine the skills you learned on the two-way skydives to produce a four point four way skydive. This section will describe a possible four-way dive from exit to breakoff that you and your coaches could use as your qualification dive.

Category 10 dive

Exit Although the exit techniques vary for each aircraft type, there are four principles that ensure exit success. These are:

1. Balanced. You must feel balanced in your exit position to make a good exit. This is achieved by ensuring your foot placement is such that it is directly underneath your centre of weight. This will allow you to launch yourself onto the relative wind.
2. Tight. Once in the door you must be close enough to the other skydivers so that you are touching, that is, shoulder to shoulder.
3. Timing. You all leave the aircraft at the same time. This is achieved by the use of an exit count which should include a verbal count (such as *ready, set, GO*), and a physical rock that can be seen or felt.
4. Presentation to the relative wind. As you launch from the aircraft you must place your chest and torso into the relative wind.

Your coaches and instructors will show you the techniques for each exit position, but these four principles provide the basis for a successful exit.

Exit specifics for a left-hand door aircraft

Middle float

Setup   Hands holding the door approximately shoulder-width apart.
Arms bent
Right foot on the edge of the door underneath the body
Left leg trailing back into the relative wind

Launch   Count and rock positively swinging left leg in and bending right knee to get push off right leg
Right hand should be the last point of contact with the aircraft

Fallaway   Arch immediately on launch
Maintain aircraft heading

Rear float

Setup   Hands toward rear edge of door
Shoulder to shoulder with middle float
Left foot on edge of door sill
Right foot hanging down below aircraft

Launch   Move with middle float on count
Drop from aircraft straight down
Right hand should be the last point of contact with the aircraft

Fallaway   Arch immediately on launch
Maintain aircraft heading

Divers

Setup   Left foot on edge of door, right foot back
Left shoulder down, right shoulder high; use right hand on top of door to ensure right shoulder high

Launch   Move with middle float on count
Push with right foot and roll over left foot
Left foot should be last point of contact with the aircraft

Fallaway   Raise thighs
             Reach arms wide and cup air
             Maintain eye contact with centre float

Freefall
The qualifying skydive will consist of the following formations:

STAR, SATELLITE, ZIG-ZAG, then back to the STAR (Figure 4.9). This figure depicts each jumper by a letter. You, the qualifier, will be skydiver D.

The first formation is the STAR and you will be directly opposite skydiver B. You will have a wrist grip on C, while A has your left wrist.

On the key, B and C will turn 45 degrees inwards and build a two-way. You will turn 45 degrees to the right and fly forward until you can pick up C's arm and leg grip. A will do the same on B.

On the key, you will turn 45 degrees left and move forward to pick up B's wrists to form a two-way. C will dock on your side and A on B's side.

On the key, fly backwards one foot and stay directly opposite B while A and C close up the star. Repeat this drill until you reach breakoff height at 3,500 feet.

Safety

At 3,500 feet you must turn and track away from the centre of the formation. Check you are clear of other skydivers and pull at 2,500 feet. As your canopy opens, check for the other canopies and be prepared to take avoiding action using your rear risers.

Congratulations; you are now a Category ten Skydiver, but remember – no one can be a champion *every* day . . .

Figure 4.9 The Category 10 qualifying dive

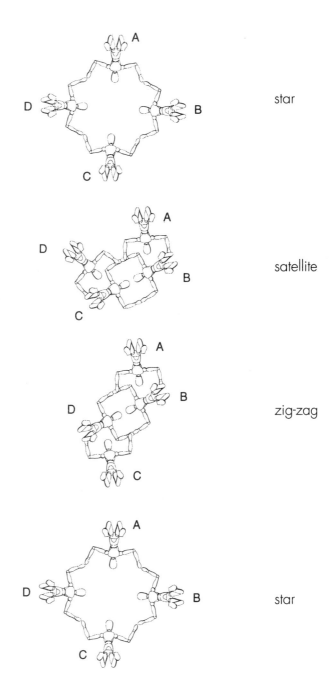

star

satellite

zig-zag

star

5 Basic Accuracy

The ability to land the parachute in a defined area is obviously important for safety reasons; we do aim, after all, always to land on the DZ and avoid those long cross-country rambles back to the clubhouse. This chapter takes canopy control a stage further and proposes that the jumper should, as a matter of course, be able to put down under normal circumstances within 10 metres of a designated target. As well as being a competition discipline, accuracy in landing is an essential prerequisite of the demonstration jumper and a fundamental skill to be mastered by all experienced parachutists. The first consideration in landing accurately is obviously that of leaving the aircraft in the correct place, and this aspect will be considered in some depth in the next chapter. Here, we are concerned with the work under the canopy.

One of the principal advantages of the Ram Air Progression System is that, because of the canopy being used, a high degree of landing precision can soon be achieved. Once you have learned to flare the canopy successfully and make consistently controlled landings, then you should always aim to put down in a precise location. In this chapter we will examine fundamental accuracy techniques as an extension to the basic canopy control lesson covered in Chapter 2 and consider these techniques in the context of competition and competition training.

 ## Safety Considerations

The target

As in all aspects of parachuting, safety must be paramount. In order to avoid injury, all accuracy training must take place into a soft landing area—a sand or gravel pit preferably at least 30 metres in diameter. There should be a windsock immediately adjacent to this area. For training purposes a distance panel should be displayed on the windline at 100 metres downwind from the target centre. The location of the pit is also important; if there are tall trees, buildings, or other solid objects nearby turbulence may be caused as the airflow (wind) is obstructed.

The canopy

Certain canopies are specifically designed for accuracy; deep section, low aspect ratio canopies, in particular the Parafoil 232, 252, and 282. This does not mean to say that very respectable scores cannot be achieved with just about any ram-air canopy—Britain's Jackie Young became the first person ever to score 10 dead centres at a World Parachute Championships in 1978 using a five cell StratoStar. So remember, it's not necessarily the canopy but the jumper flying it that counts. **You** can learn to put your canopy down exactly where you wish.

When you start training, however, it is essential that you are jumping a canopy that cannot be stalled

Handling the canopy

Accuracy jumping is all about smooth canopy control. In particular, you **must** turn the canopy into wind by 300ft and you must not make any violent manoeuvres, that is, rapid and excessive control movements, below this height.

An Accuracy Briefing

Let us now run through the sequence of events which an accuracy jump entails. The jump starts as you arrive at the DZ; you should be alert to the prevailing conditions and already mentally considering your tactics. The factors to be considered are:

Wind: Speed
               Direction
               Gusting or steady
Temperature: High temperatures give rise to thermals and associated turbulence. Cool, stable conditions are best for accuracy jumping.

Pre-jump actions

Observation   A Wind Drift Indicator is always thrown on the first lift of the day. You should observe the WDI preferably from the target. Check that it was thrown accurately, directly overhead. It is a good idea to time it. It should take between 100 and 120 seconds to land. Remember, there are always so many variables in a parachute descent it is good practice to eliminate as many of them as possible. So make sure you know the opening point and the wind line. Having watched the WDI you should also be observing the other jumpers; this is particularly important in high wind conditions; what are the upper winds doing? Is there a change in direction? If so, at what height? Observe the angle at which the other jumpers descend on to the target. Have they any difficulty getting in from their selected setup point? All of these indicators will assist you in forming your plan.

Your equipment   Ensure that your harness is snug and well-fitting, with no loose webbing, clothing or anything else flapping to cause a distraction. Make sure your altimeter—wrist or chest mount—is clearly visible. Check your own equipment thoroughly before putting it on and do not rely passively on a flight-line check. (You should be doing this as a matter of routine by now anyway).

The plan Your plan should be formulated before emplaning as a result of your observations. Decide your exit point, take into account any extreme wind conditions, and decide your **setup point** (Table 5.1). This setup point will be modified during the descent as a result of your own observations under canopy. In some cases you will not be doing your own spotting. This does not mean you take no interest in the process. You must at least know where the opening point is in order to take appropriate remedial action (run, hold, crab etc) if the spot is off.

Table 5.1: Setup distances, height 300ft, flying 50% brakes

Windspeed		Distance
Calm		100 metres
Light	1–3 m/sec	50 metres
Medium	4–5 m/sec	25 metres
Strong	6–7 m/sec	0–10 metres

The jump

Accuracy jumps are normally made from between 2,500ft and 3,500ft. If you are still a Student jumper, you should be making a 5 second delay from 3,500ft. This means you will be open high and exposed to (possibly) stronger upper wind conditions; take your time, and exit deep. Once the canopy is open, do your safety checks, locate the DZ and assess your own position in relation to the target and the ideal opening point.

Control mode Relax in the harness and fly the canopy generally on half brakes most of the time. This means that the canopy is flying more slowly, is more responsive and gives you a reserve of speed and brakes. The only time you should be on full drive is if you are too close and have to hold or are too far away and need the canopy speed to get you back. Once you are happy with your position in relation to the target, go back on to half brakes.

The objective   In an accuracy jump, 90 per cent of your time under canopy has but one objective: to get you to the **correct setup point.** The setup point may be defined as the horizontal distance from the target at a height of 300ft from which you can descend onto the disc on 50–75 per cent brakes with minimum corrections. In other words, from this point, the angle from 300ft to the disc should remain constant. Therefore, be positive, fly the canopy all the time with purpose. Spend the time from opening height to about 2,000ft flying the canopy around and continuously assessing your drift. At about 2,000ft, turn the canopy into wind and check penetration (that is, the extent to which you are making ground into wind, if any) on 50 per cent brakes. This will help you decide your setup point. As you gain experience, another penetration check can be carried out at 1,000ft.

The approach (Figure 5.1)   From about 1500ft fly the canopy on 50 per cent brakes downwind to your parking zone. The landing pattern you were originally taught can be modified from now on. Fly your pattern about 100–150 metres to the side of the target. It is a good idea to establish either a right hand or a left hand pattern which you will use every time (with rare exceptions when you are forced to take a certain line). This will mean that you see the same picture each time you turn in. Eliminate as many variables as possible.

At about 1,000ft turn crosswind about 50 metres deeper than your planned setup distance and establish a parking zone behind the target. Use short S turns to wash off your height. Observe the windsock at the pit and manoeuvre so that you are exactly into wind at

Figure 5.1 A basic accuracy approach

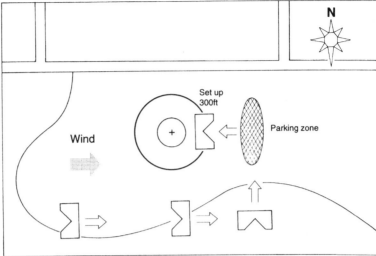

300ft at the required distance out (Table 5.1). Always aim to set up at the same height. Again, eliminate as many variables as possible.

The setup   A setup height of 300ft will give you 20–25 seconds on finals. This is long enough for you to make adjustments, but not too long for you to lose concentration. Assuming you are flying about half brakes on finals, Table 5.1 gives approximate distances for a 300ft setup point.

Note
To conform with international practice, and as we are dealing in seconds it simplifies the calculations if we convert knots to metres/second. 1m/sec. = 2 knots.

Working speed   You are already familiar with the concepts of **groundspeed** and **airspeed** from your canopy control lesson in Chapter 2. In accuracy jumping we are concerned with a **working speed**. Working speed is the ground speed which is selected by use of brakes and on final approach should ideally be maintained at about 2m/sec. This working speed will perforce vary in extreme conditions as the limits of the canopy's performance are reached.

Finals As you turn in on finals, take a deep breath, relax, and concentrate on the disc. Sit comfortably in the harness. Canopy, head, and body should all be in the same vertical line; legs comfortably apart, arms shoulder width apart and toggles level in the half brake position with the elbows naturally bent. Legs or arms out of plumb will cause the canopy to slide. There must be no movement in the harness, only the hands should move. Your task now is by use of brakes to keep the angle to the disc constant. Make sure you are directly on the wind line, if you find you are slipping off to one side, correct by a small elevation/depression turn and always face the disc. Finally, fly the canopy right down to the disc; in other words do not make any premature strikes in the general direction of the pad but concentrate on precise foot placement. The most accurate strikes are made with the heel. Finally **never give up** on your approach.

Landings As you will have appreciated by now, we are not asking for a full speed approach for the last 100 feet coupled with a flared landing. You can quite safely land a student canopy on 50–100 per cent brakes onto a soft target area without risk of injury. It is imperative that you are using a canopy that cannot be stalled. Safety must always remain paramount; if, for example you are on deep brakes and are undershooting, do not let up suddenly. Remember all canopy handling below 300ft must be non-violent. Never risk injury for the sake of a few metres or centimetres. If you are outside the scoring area at this stage, take the easy landing, work out, (or ask) where you went wrong and concentrate on the next jump. At least you'll still be around to make it.

Jumping in competition

Team jumping In competition, the accuracy event is performed as a four or five person team jump. The exit order is determined primarily by weight, with the heaviest jumper out first. Ideally, this should also be the most experienced jumper. The leader should fast fall and make the maximum legal delay; the others should exit at reasonable intervals to ensure vertical and horizontal separation. Delays from 3,500ft should be of the order 10 seconds, 8, 5, and 3. Once your canopy is open, do your safety checks, locate the DZ and assess your own position in relation to the target and the ideal opening point. Each competitor should be able to make an individual approach to the target, and everybody should go the same way round. Remember that in a team stack, the low canopy always has right of way.

Competition rules   The rules for the Team and Individual Accuracy Events which were approved by the International Parachuting Commission (IPC) in 1995 are reproduced at Annex B to this Manual.

6 Spotting

The ability to spot the aircraft is a requirement for the FAI C Certificate (British Standard) which reads:

'C' Certificate: Category 10, 50 descents, cleared for spotting and has been briefed on the responsibilities of being a Jumpmaster.

It has been claimed that the advent in 1972 of the ram-air canopy in Britain signalled the demise of the art of spotting. The facts are that, prior to 1972, the fastest canopy available was the Paracommander type, with an airspeed of about 10mph (4 m/sec). This gave a theoretical opening zone radius of 480 metres and a safe opening zone radius of half this. In reality, you had to open the canopy within 200 metres of the ideal opening point to guarantee being in the right field. The ram-air concept changed all this; with canopies now capable of speeds easily in excess of 20mph (9 m/sec) this opening zone has now been dramatically enlarged to a circle some 2,000 metres in diameter.

Nevertheless, the single most important factor in accurate parachuting remains the exit point, universally referred to as the spot. The responsibility of the jumpmaster is to spot the load correctly, and while for most of us the spot may not be so crucial to the final result as it once was, leaving the aircraft at the correct point remains a fundamental requirement for an accurate landing. It must also be remembered that there are still a lot of students jumping round canopies who need all the help they can get.

There are two separate skills in spotting: the first is working out the correct exit point and the second, which requires more practise, is getting the aeroplane to fly over it. Both skills will be considered in turn; first the calculations.

The calculations

In determining the exit point, the three factors that have to be taken into consideration are **projection** or **throw-forward, freefall drift**, and **canopy drift**. Let us look at each of these in turn. As in the previous chapter we will work in metres per second, using 1m/sec = 2kt.

Throw-forward   The throw-forward is calculated by an empirical formula based on the true air speed (TAS) of the jump aircraft. Throw-forward only becomes a truly important factor in high-altitude jumping (20,000ft plus), but will nevertheless be considered here as a factor in the equation.

The formula is: $P = \dfrac{5VT}{T+5}$

where V = aircraft TAS in m/sec
T = length of delay in seconds (calculated to 10 seconds)

Using a TAS of 60kt or 30m/sec, we have the following result:

$$P = \frac{5 \times 30 \times 10}{(10+5)} = \frac{1500}{15} = 100 \text{ metres } \textbf{projection}$$

Freefall drift   Drift in freefall is calculated by multiplying the time in freefall (seconds) by the mean windspeed (expressed in m/sec) from drop height to opening height.

Canopy drift   Canopy drift is similarly calculated by multiplying the time under canopy by the mean windspeed expressed in m/sec. However, whereas both throw-forward and freefall drift have been calculated in advance before emplaning, selection of the **opening point**, as opposed to the **exit point** must be made with regard to actual, rather than forecast, conditions.

The most common and reliable method of doing this is to drop a Wind Drift Indicator (WDI) at a height of 2,000ft above the target, time it, mark its landing position, and transpose the distance covered on a reciprocal bearing upwind of the target. This is the **opening point**. The WDI should be in the air for about 110–120 seconds. It must be timed if an accurate opening point is to be plotted.

We will now take a worked example based on the following set of data:

AIRCRAFT SPEED	60kt (30m/sec)
DROPPING HEIGHT	12, 000ft AGL
OPENING HEIGHT	2,000ft AGL
DELAYED FALL	60 seconds
WINDS—MEAN SPEED	12, 000ft–2,000ft
AND DIRECTION	290°/20kt (10m/sec)
	2,000ft-surface
	220°/12kt (6m/sec)

Note:

A met. forecast will express wind direction in degrees true, whereas aircraft fly on magnetic headings; for working purposes the small deviation involved can be safely ignored.

The method

1. Mark the freefall drift on the airphoto as a vector
2. Throw the WDI at 2,000ft over the target
3. Mark the position of the WDI and the opening point on the airphoto
4. Draw in the windline
5. Lay off the freefall drift vector to produce an exit point, allowing 100 metres short for the throwforward.

Figure 6.1 illustrates this worked example.

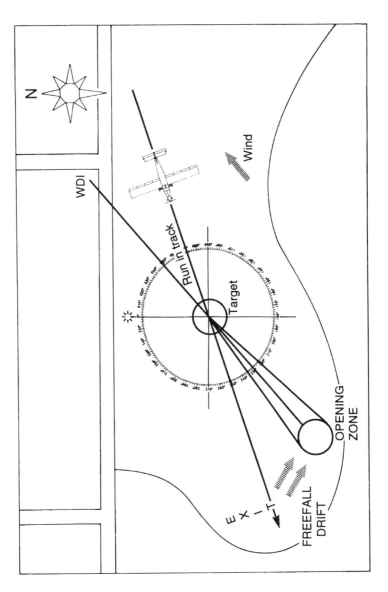

Figure 6.1 Calculation of opening and exit points

Wind cones and opening zones

The opening point, as indicated by the WDI, is the theoretical point from which an unmodified canopy would drift on to the target. The inherent drive of a modified, or of a ram-air, canopy makes it more realistic to think in terms of an opening zone, rather than a geometrical point. The wind cone is an imaginary three-dimensional figure within which the parachutist must remain in order to land on the target (Figure 6.2). If the jumper strays outside this cone, he will be unable to make the target.

The opening zone radius is determined by the airspeed of the canopy and consequently varies with the type of canopy used. This radius is the product of the canopy airspeed in m/sec and the time in the air. Assuming this time is 120 seconds from opening height the following opening zone radii may be calculated:

Canopy type

Student round	Airspeed 3m/sec × 120 sec = 360 metre radius
Student ram-air	Airspeed 8m/sec × 120 sec = 960 metre radius
High performance ram-air	Airspeed 12m/sec × 120 sec = 1440 metre radius

These, of course, are theoretical limits, presupposing constant windspeeds and allowing no latitude at all in the handling of the canopy. A safer opening zone is an area 25 per cent of the theoretical maximum, as indicated in Figure 6.2.

Accurate parachuting results from an intelligent study of the prevailing meteorological conditions and consequent application to each aircraft load. This met. information is available each day from Air Traffic Control (ATC) or the local area Met. Office and should be used in conjunction with the WDI to keep everybody, even if not on the target, at least on the airfield.

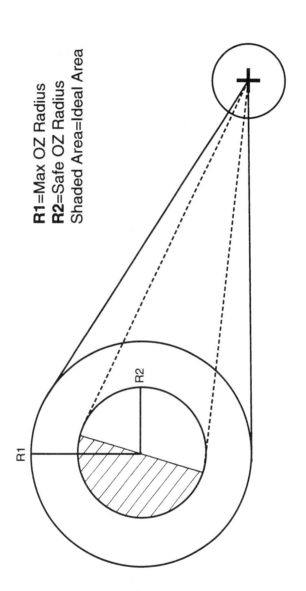

R1=Max OZ Radius
R2=Safe OZ Radius
Shaded Area=Ideal Area

R1

R2

Figure 6.2 Wind cones

The application

Having worked out our opening point and exit point, we now come to the application of this knowledge in getting the aircraft to fly the line we need to get there. Spotting is a skill that needs practice; it involves co-operation between the jumpmaster and the pilot and an appreciation by each of the problems of the other.

Thus, the first job of the jumpmaster is to brief the pilot on exactly what is required; that is:

Run in heading(s)
Number of passes
Heights of passes
Numbers out of each pass
Static line or freefall
Types of exit (floaters etc)
Total number on board
Whether the jumpmaster is jumping or not.

At our own Centre, the pilot is given a copy of the manifest; failing this the pilot usually notes down details of the load. Once airborne, communication is more difficult, and a good briefing will prevent mis-understandings and frustration. There is nothing more unprofessional than an argument between jumpmaster and pilot at altitude.

First principles

WDI observation The WDI must be thrown directly above the target at a height of 2,000ft. This WDI pass is normally made into wind. The pilot should then fly a left hand circuit if the jumpmaster is operating out of a left-hand door and a right hand circuit if the starboard door is being used. The pilot should also make every effort to observe the WDI. The jumpmaster must **concentrate** on watching the WDI as under hazy conditions it can easily be lost. The same applies when the WDI is thrown over a built-up area as for example on a demo. Spare WDIs should always be kept in the aircraft. If there is any doubt where the WDI landed, another should be thrown.

The wind line Once the WDI has landed, the jump-master takes an imaginary line from its landing point through the target to a prominent ground feature equidistant upwind of the target. This feature is the opening point. The imaginary line is the wind line, and is the ideal ground track the aircraft should follow when jumping from low altitudes or when there is little significant lateral upper drift.

Aircraft heading and aircraft ground track The jumpmaster is concerned with an imaginary line drawn on the ground, and he must ensure the aircraft is following this line. Because of the effect of winds at altitude, the aircraft heading may be significantly different from this ground track and it is important that the jumpmaster appreciates this (Figure 6.3).

Figure 6.3
Aircraft heading
and aircraft
ground track

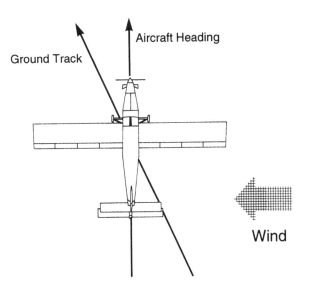

Aircraft attitude The aircraft must be flying straight and level, in order that the true vertical can be observed. If the aircraft is spotted in the climb, the

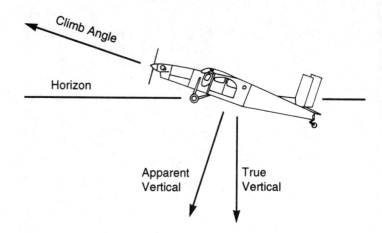

Figure 6.4
Influence of air-
craft climb angle
on the spot

apparent vertical will be too far ahead, and the
jumpers will leave too early (Figure 6.4). If the aircraft
is banking to the left, the apparent vertical will be to
the right and vice versa (Figure 6.5). Ten degrees of
bank at 12,000ft can cause a lateral error of up to 700
metres.

This principle of accurate vertical observation
applies with equal force to the jumpmaster himself; in
other words he must be certain he is looking directly
downwards. A common fault is leaning too far out of
the door with a corresponding loss of vertical perspec-

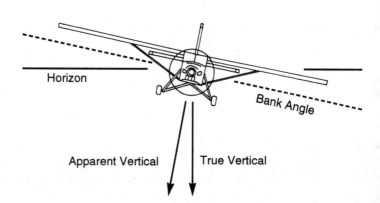

Figure 6.5
Influence of air-
craft bank angle
on the spot

tive. In both these cases, the greater the altitude, the greater the magnification of error.

Reaction times Failure to appreciate this factor is probably the biggest single element in producing a bad spot. It applies particularly to FS groups where floaters and climb out are involved. Remember even at 70kt, the aircraft is covering 35 metres every second and due allowance must be made for this.

Giving corrections Corrections are given to the pilot either by hand signals or by lights on the instrument panel from the jumpmaster's control buttons. It is a good idea for the pilot to utilise a rear-view mirror to maintain eye contact with the jumpmaster. Corrections are understood to be in five degree increments. The pilot should keep the turns as flat as possible, using rudder and opposite aileron, to preserve the jump-master's vertical vision. Once the correction is given, the pilot will remain on the new heading. Thus, if the jumpmaster wishes to take the aircraft on a parallel track, say 200 metres to port, he will give a left correc-tion, followed by a right correction once the aircraft has moved over sufficiently. Once the correction has been given, time should be allowed for the revised run-in to be assessed. Finally, corrections should not be given in cloud as the pilot has enough to handle in just flying the aeroplane.

The jump run When running in, it is essential for safety reasons that the pilot indicates this fact to the jumpmaster. This means, (1) that the pilot has been given **clear drop** from DZ Control and (2) that the air-craft is in the correct dropping configuration and at the correct dropping speed. The jumpmaster must con-centrate on keeping the aircraft on his pre-determined run-in track toward the exit point, which may be at some variance with the opening point if there is any appreciable freefall drift.

Calling the exit The jumpmaster **must** make up his mind where the exit is to be called. The main

considerations are reaction times for student parachutists and climb out times for FS groups, also aircraft
ground speed and throwforward, particularly if a
downwind run is being made. He may wish to call a
cut to the pilot to reduce power; this is a pretty common practice and is obviously an indication to the pilot
that the exit is imminent.

Once the cut has been called, the jumpmaster should
then concentrate solely on what is happening inside
the aircraft. As he is ultimately responsible for the
load, he should exit last in order to supervise all the
jumpers all the time.

Other considerations

Parallax effect   This is 'the angular amount of apparent displacement of an object, caused by the actual
change of point of observation' (*Concise Oxford
Dictionary*). Parallax is what makes it virtually impos-
sible to determine the actual landing point of a canopy
(or WDI) from the air until the said canopy or WDI has
actually touched down. Important to remember when
observing previous jumpers with a view to changing
the run-in/spot.

Cloud   Parachutists may not leave an aircraft if at the
point of exit the ground between the opening point
and the intended landing area is not visible. (Ops.
Manual Section 8.3.(a)). This is an obvious safety consideration and particularly important for student
jumpers in the early stages. Sometimes cloud which
may be a problem at 3,000ft will no longer be so at
higher altitude. In addition, if there is patchy cloud
over the opening point, the run-in may be adjusted to
one side or the other to avoid it, relying on the canopy
capability to make up the error. Alternatively, crosswind or downwind passes can be made to give the
jumpmaster better sight of the DZ.

Crosswind pass   Cloud reasons apart, crosswind
passes are mainly used on student dropping from rel-

Figure 6.6 A crosswind pass

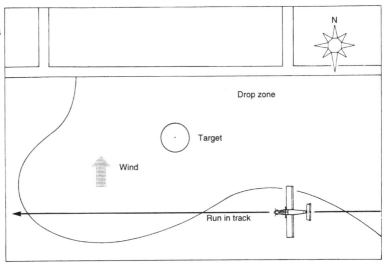

atively low altitudes when the wind direction and orientation of the Drop Zone make this a safer option. Factors to be considered include DZ hazards and number of jumpers out on each pass (Figure 6.6). Student jumpers should be pre-briefed on the change of conventional run-in.

Downwind pass   Downwind passes are mainly used by Style jumpers in training and competition. The object of the jump is to gain vertical speed immediately on exit and to perform a set of manoeuvres facing the ground-to-air video camera. A downwind run is therefore chosen so this target is in view from the outset. The exit point must be calculated carefully because of the increased groundspeed of the aircraft and the throw forward.

On rare occasions it may be necessary to make a downwind pass for an accuracy jump. Under such conditions, the team stack must be reversed, with delays of 3, 5, 8 and 10 seconds (see Chapter 5: **Team jumping**).

In conclusion

Success in spotting, as in all parachuting skills, is the result of a sound understanding of the basic principles involved and constant practise in applying them under varying conditions. Just as every jump is different, and there is something to be learned from each one, so it is with the control of an aircraft load. Different types of aircraft, different Drop Zones, differing weather conditions, different types of jumper, different pilots, the permutations are endless. Never be afraid to ask questions, never be afraid to take responsibility. The safe and accurate delivery of an aircraft load of jumpers from altitude onto a tight DZ under marginal conditions is one of the most rewarding experiences the sport has to offer. As we said in the Introduction to this Manual:

GO FOR IT; AND REMEMBER—YOU'LL NEVER GET GOOD IN THE AIR IF YOU ALWAYS STAY ON THE GROUND.

Operations Manual, Section 8, Parachute Limitations

1. General

Parachuting may only take place under the conditions laid out in the BPA Operations Manual. Variations or amendments to the requirements of the Operations Manual must be subject of formal application to and acceptance by the Council of the British Parachute Association, usually via the Safety and Training Committee (STC).

NB 1. Memorandum and Articles of Association for the BPA can be obtained from the BPA Office.
NB 2. Terms of Reference and Rules of Procedure for STC can be found on BPA Form 160.

2. Wind

(a) Ground windspeed limits for parachutists are as follows:
(i)   Student Parachutists jumping round parachutes 10 knots
(ii) Student Parachutists jumping ram-air parachutes 15 knots
(iii) Parachutists, Experienced Parachutists and Tandem parachutists   20 knots

(b) Suspension and resumption of parachuting. Suspension of parachuting will be ordered for the designations of parachutists concerned after two gusts above the limit have taken place within five minutes.

After parachuting has been suspended it will not be resumed for at least thirty minutes during which time no gusts above the limit have occurred.

(c) Every club must use an anemometer for measuring ground wind speed.

(d) The strength and direction of winds below 2,000 feet AGL will be indicated by the use of Wind Drift Indicators (WDIs).

(e) A WDI must be dropped:
(i)   Before parachuting begins
(ii)   Following a significant change in wind velocity or direction
(iii) Following any break of more than thirty minutes caused by winds in excess of the limits laid down (see sub para (a) above).
(iv) After parachutists have failed to land in the intended landing area and a faulty spot or bad canopy control is not suspected.

3. Cloud and visibility

(a) **Cloud**. Parachutists may not leave an aircraft if at the point of exit the ground between the opening point and the intended landing area is not visible.
(b) **Visibility**. The minimum flight visibility must be at least 5km.

4. Opening heights

The minimum height that parachutists must have their main parachutes open by are as follows:

(a) Student Parachutists jumping round parachutes 2,000ft AGL

(b) Student Parachutists jumping ram-air parachutes 3,000ft AGL

(c) Parachutists and Experienced Parachutists 2,000ft AGL

(d) Tandem parachutists 5,000ft AGL

(e) FAI 'D' Certificate holders on displays 1,500ft AGL

5. Maximum altitude

(a) Normal parachuting will not take place above 12,000ft AGL

(b) Parachuting will only take place between 12,000ft and 15,000ft AGL without oxygen provided that:
(i)   The aircraft when loaded with parachutists can sustain at least 1,000 feet per minute rate of climb between 10,000 and 15,000 feet.
(ii) No parachuting lift exposes parachutists to altitudes above 12,000 feet for more than six minutes.
(iii) The DZ height AMSL does not exceed 500 feet

(c) Clubs or members who wish to parachute above 15,000 AGL (with oxygen) will need STC approval and must submit their plans and details of their equipment in advance.

6. Cutaways

(a) Parachutists and Experienced Parachutists my perform a cutaway at their DZ with a cutaway rig designed for the purpose, provided they have CCI approval and have been thoroughly drilled in the cutaway procedures.

(b) Display cutaways will only be performed by FAI 'D' Certificate holders when a cutaway rig designed for the purpose is being used.

7. Number of parachutists per pass

(a) No more than three Traditional (round canopy) or two RAPS static line Student Parachutists will be despatched per pass over the DZ.

(b) No more than four Traditional or two RAPS freefall Student Parachutists will be despatched per pass over the DZ.

8. Water jumps

Water jumps may only be made in the following conditions:

(a) When there is a minimum of one power boat for each parachutist in the air.

(b) When all parachutists are equipped with suitable buoyancy aids and have been briefed on their use.

(c) When DZ Control is organised by an Advanced Instructor who must be present during the entire programme.

9. Night jumps

(a) Category 8 and 50 jumps is the minimum qualification to take part in a night descent.

(b) Drop Zone Control must be organised by an Advanced Instructor, who must be present during the entire programme.

(c) All parachutists are to be briefed on the position of all obstructions adjacent to the DZ.

(d) The DZ is to be marked in a standardized manner (Figure B 1).

(e) Any obstructions within the DZ are to be lit.

(f) The DZ must be indicated to the parachutists by the jumpmaster from the air prior to exit.

(g) Torches are to be available for use inside the aircraft.

(h) All parachutists must have at least one light.

(i) The pilot is to be in communication with local ATC.

(j) Local police are to be informed of proposed night descents.

(k) Notification of night parachuting is to be made in writing at least five working days in advance to:

Airspace Utilisation Section
National Air Traffic Services
Hillingdon House
Uxbridge, Middlesex, UB10 0RU
Tel: 01895 276108
Fax: 01895 276142

Giving the following information:
(i)   Name, address and telephone number of Club
(ii) Name of CCI
(iii) Date and time of proposed night parachuting
(iv) Name of DZ, together with six-figure grid refer-
      ence, using OS 1:50,000 series
(v)   Proposed dropping height.

Figure B 1

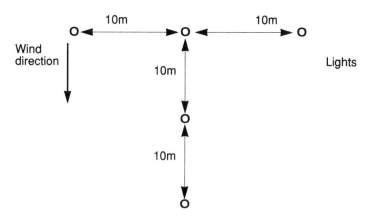

Competition Rules
(Approved by the IPC in January 1995)

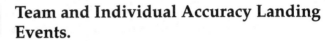

Team and Individual Accuracy Landing Events.

5.1.1 Wind Drift Indicator

(1) Prior to starting the event, or if jumping has been interrupted for more than thirty (30) minutes, at least one wind drift indicator must be dropped from an altitude 100m below the exit altitude and above the target by a judge or by an experienced parachutist appointed by the Chief or Event Judge.

(2) The wind drift indicator must have approximately the same rate of descent as the parachutes used by most of the competitors. Its landing point must be marked on an aerial photo or plan of the Drop Zone.

(3) Continuity of the event and the opportunity for competitors to observe canopies in the air is considered sufficient for all competitors to evaluate the opening point.

5.1.2 Exit Point

Each competitor or team selects their own exit point.

5.1.3 Wind Speed

The maximum allowable wind speed at ground level in the accuracy events is 7m/sec. Scoring must stop while the wind exceeds this limit and for a period of 30 seconds after the wind has returned below 7m/sec. Scoring may then resume. The event will be automatically interrupted if the ground wind speed exceeds 9m/sec.

5.1.4 Wind Direction on the Ground

(1) The windsock must be capable of responding to winds of at least 2m/sec. It should have a minimum length of 4m and a minimum diameter at the inlet of 600mm. The judges will determine its location, which is at a fixed place approximately 50m from the target centre. This decision is not subject to any protest.

(2) A wind direction indicator (streamer) mounted on a pole, which is capable of responding to winds of less than 2m/sec will be placed by the Event Judge within the 25m circle.

5.1.5 Target

(1) The centre of the target must be an Automatic Measuring Device with a Dead Centre Disc of 5cm diameter in a contrasting colour, preferably yellow on a black background. The device must be kept as flat as possible, and capable of measuring to a minimum distance of 15cm.

(2) The Automatic Measuring Device is mounted centrally on an underlying pad of at least 1.2m diameter which when struck scores 16cm at all points.

(3) The Automatic Measuring Device and the underlying pad are placed centrally on an artificial pit, which has the following specifications:

diameter:	approx 5m
thickness:	a minimum of 30cm
compressibility:	0.15–0.20 kp/sq cm
colour:	grey

(4) Clearly marked circles of 0.5m (only if there is a control pad), 10m and 25m radius, centred round the dead centre disc.

(5) The Automatic Measuring Device must be

repositioned immediately after the landing of any competitor who moves or covers its location, except during team jumps when there is insufficient time between the landing of the team members.

(6) In order not to damage the Automatic Measuring Device, suitable footwear must be worn.

5.1.6 Presence on the Target

(1) The only persons allowed within the 25 metre circle during jumping are the members of the Panel of Judges, members of the Jury and necessary members of the organising staff.

(2) Team managers, accredited press, radio and television officials, and guests of the Organisers are allowed in a reserved area of the 25 metre circle designated by the Event Judge and not closer than 15 metres to the Automatic Measuring Device.

(3) During the final approach of a competitor, only members of the Panel of Judges are allowed within 5 metres. Exceptions to this rule are the responsibility of the Chief Judge.

(4) After a landing, competitors must leave the target area immediately.

5.1.7 Rejumps

(1) Any malfunction of the main parachute canopy which creates a control problem for a competitor may merit a rejump. In this case the competitor must indicate immediately that he has such a problem by signalling with his arms or legs outstretched, or other suitable signal, throughout most of the descent and must make no attempt to land in the target area. Following a malfunction, the inspection of the equipment immediately after the competitor has landed must indicate that the competitor did suffer a malfunction that was not created by the competitor himself.

(2) A control problem is a condition in the deployment of the parachute such that it is virtually impossi-

ble to attempt a precision target approach, or that the main canopy configuration is such as to prevent the competitor from demonstrating his skill.

(3) If there is a sudden change in ground wind direction of more than 90 degrees when the wind speed is more than 3m/sec during the final approach of a competitor a rejump must be offered. The judges at the target decide if the competitor is on final approach. Their decision is no grounds for a protest.

(4) If, during the accuracy events, two or more competitors approach and/or land on the target simultaneously or close together, and in the process interfere with each other, a rejump for one, or both, or neither may be awarded. If such an interference occurs between members of the same team during team accuracy jumps, no rejump will be granted.

(5) If an Automatic Measuring Device is found to be defective or not reset and the first point of contact has been on it, and (4) above does not apply, the affected competitor(s) must be offered a rejump.

(6) If the Automatic Measuring Device registers a score and in the opinion of the judges at the target the first point of contact was not on the Automatic Measuring Device, the competitor will not be granted a rejump, and must receive a score of 16cm.

(7) Only the affected competitors will make a rejump and get a new score, the rejump counting for both the individual and team accuracy events. The exit altitude for rejumps will be decided by the Meet Director and be between 700 and 1100m.

5.1.8 Scoring Accuracy Landing

(1) The landing point is the first point of body contact with the ground or the Automatic Measuring Device.

(2) The Automatic Measuring Device must register the distance between the landing point and the edge of the dead centre disc where the landing point is on the Automatic Measuring Device.

(3) Any landing point off the Automatic Measuring Device must be given a score of 16cm.

(4) Teams jumping with less than 5 members must receive a score of 16cm for each missing member.

(5) Any jump-off for tied places is made with an Automatic Measuring Device having a Dead Centre Disc of 3cm diameter.

(6) The five scores of each round shall be the score for the team for that round, unless one or more members of the team were disqualified for that round.

(7) If, because of insufficient separation between team members, a competitor lands on the Automatic Measuring Device which has not been reset the score given is 15cm. Competitors landing off the Automatic Measuring Device will be given the score of 16cm.

5.1.9 Team Accuracy Landing Event

(1) A team consists of a maximum of 5 members. All 5 scores will count in the team event.

(2) A team with less than three members will jump in mixed teams at the end of each round. Members from different countries will be treated as individual contestants only.

(3) The exit altitude is 1100 metres. The team must jump from the same aircraft, during the same passage of the aircraft over the target (rejumps are treated as individual jumps). If meteorological conditions do not allow jumping from 1100 metres, the altitude may be lowered to 900 metres for a whole round.

(4) The jump order may only be changed to allow for repacking, to accommodate rejumps and to avoid competition delays resulting from substantial changes in the order of jumping.

5.1.10 Individual Accuracy Landing Events

(1) Scores for all rounds except the semi-final and final rounds, are the scores obtained in the team accuracy jumps.

(2) Semi-final and final jumps are as individuals, and must be made from as high an altitude as possible between 700 and 800 metres.

Glossary

AAD	Automatic activation device, normally used in conjunction with the reserve parachute as a backup system. Mandatory for RAPS students. *See* CYPRES, FXC, Sentinel.
Accuracy	Competition discipline; target is a 3 or 5cm diameter disc in the centre of an electronic measuring device.
AFF	Accelerated Free Fall. Training system involving altitude freefall from the first jump under the physical guidance of two instructors.
AGL	Above Ground Level.
Airtech GmbH	*See* CYPRES.
AMD	Automatic Measuring Device. Developed and manufactured by Gerd Weckbecker, Lechstrasse 25, D 86978 Hohenfurch, Germany. Tel: (49) 8861 7859.
AMSL	Above Mean Sea Level.
Angle of attack	The angle between the relative airflow and the chord line of the ram-air canopy. Denoted by the Greek letter alpha.
Angle of incidence	The fixed angle of canopy trim (usually 13 degrees) resulting from the differential A and D suspension line lengths. Denoted by the Greek letter phi. *See* p. 33.
ANO	Air Navigation Order. ANO Article 49 (1) and (5) permits Sport Parachuting within the UK provided that the requirements of the Operations Manual are complied with.
APA	Army Parachute Association (Netheravon). Airfield Camp, Netheravon, Salisbury, Wilts, SP4 9SF. Tel: 01980 678277 .
Aspect ratio	The ratio between the span and the chord of a wing, or of a ram-air canopy.

B4	Type of US Air Force surplus container and harness.
Base	Formation Skydiving terminology. Denotes the passive jumper or jumpers with whom contact is made when building a formation. Cf Pin.
BASE jumping	Fixed-object jumping (Buildings, Antennae, Spans, Earth).
BOC	Bottom of Container. (Position for hand-deployed pilot chute).
BPA	British Parachute Association. 5 Wharf Way, Glen Parva, Leicester, LE2 9TF. Tel: 0116 278 5271.
Bridle line	Line attaching pilot chute to canopy or deployment bag.
Burble	Zone of turbulent air immediately above/behind a freefalling jumper or formation of jumpers. Also ram-air canopy wake.
CAA	Civil Aviation Authority, Aviation House, Gatwick Airport South, W. Sussex RH6 0YR. Tel: 01293 567171.
Canopy release	Device to disconnect risers from main harness. *See* Three ring, Capewell.
Canopy stack	*See* CRW.
Capewell	Canopy release, manufactured by Capewell, of Hartford, Connecticut USA; pre-dates Three ring.
CCI	Club Chief Instructor.
Chord	The length of the chord line of an aerofoil. Cf Span.
Chord line	Straight line joining the leading edge to the trailing edge of the aerofoil.
CISM	Conseil International du Sport Militaire. International Military Sports Council. Organises annual Military World Sport Parachuting Championships.
Crabbing	Flying canopy crosswind (normally on full drive).
Cross-port venting	System of vents cut in the ribs of ram-air canopies to ensure even pressurisation.

CRW	Canopy Relative Work. Two or more jumpers linking or working closely together in various configurations under open canopies. Designated Canopy Formation as a competition discipline.
Cutaway	To release main canopy (Normally carried out in the event of a partial malfunction). *See* Three ring.
CYPRES	Cybernetic Parachute Release System. Automatic activation device developed and manufactured by: Airtec GmbH, Mittelstrasse 69, D 33181 Wünnenberg, Germany. Tel: (49) 2953 8010 *See* p. 53.
DC	Dead Centre accuracy landing.
Diaper	Fabric deployment device integral with the lower lateral band of (usually) a round reserve canopy on which the suspension lines are stowed. Acts as a mouth lock to ensure line-first deployment.
Dirt Dive	Ground rehearsal for a Formation Skydive.
Disc	Target dead centre, 3 or 5 cm in diameter.
Downplane	CRW manoeuvre involving two or more jumpers linked by legs flying canopies with leading edges facing the ground; that is, straight down.
DRCP	Dummy ripcord pull. Exercise carried out on static line jump in preparation for first freefall.
Drogue	Small canopy used to slow and stabilise the jumper, or other load. Used in tandem jumping.
Dytter	Audible height alarm. Manufactured by Larsen & Brusgaard, Mosevej 3, Kirke Hyllinge 4070 Denmark. Tel: (45) 42 40 44 05.
DZ	Dropping Zone.
Extractor	*See* Pilot chute.
FAA	Federal Aviation Administration (USA). Cf CAA (UK).

FAI	Fédération Aéronautique Internationale. World Governing Body of Aviation Sport. 93 boulevard du Montparnasse, 75006 Paris. Tel: (33) 1 49 54 38 92.
Flare	1. Triangular segment of nylon fabric attaching suspension lines to canopy seams to dissipate the opening shock load. 2. Landing technique in which the speed of a ram-air canopy is traded for lift just before touch-down.
Floater	Jumper positioned outside aircraft prior to FS exit.
Frap hat	Lightweight leather protective helmet of French design.
Free bag	Deployment bag for a ram-air reserve canopy. Unattached to the canopy in order to prevent horseshoe type malfunctions of the reserve.
Front mount	Type of reserve container attached to the front of the jumper's harness by two snaphooks.
FS	Formation Skydiving (Competition Relative Work) *See* RW.
FXC 12000	Automatic Activation Device. *See* p. 52.
FXC Corporation	AAD Manufacturer. 3410 S. Susan Street, Santa Ana, California 92704–6997, USA. Tel: (1) 714 556 7400.
GATW	Good All The Way. Instructor critique in logbook entry.
GQ	UK parachute manufacturing company formed in 1932. (James Gregory and Raymond Quilter) GQ Parachutes Ltd., Isfryn Industrial Estate, Blackmill, Mid Glam. CF35 6EB. Tel: 01656 840300.
HAHO	High Altitude High Opening. Military tactical standoff delivery. *See* Standoff.
HALO	High Altitude Low Opening. Military tactical freefall.
Hand deploy	Hand deployed pilot chute (as opposed to spring-loaded pilot chute). May be used

	only by Cat 8 jumpers and above. *See* Throwaway.
Hangup	Parachutist accidentally caught up outside aircraft, usually on jammed static line. *See* p. 31.
Hogback	*See* Piggyback.
Holding	Facing canopy into wind on full drive.
IPC	International Parachuting Commission. Sub-Committee of the FAI. Responsible to the FAI for all parachuting matters, including the organisation of WPCs.
Irvin	Leslie Leroy Irvin. American test jumper and parachute designer. Made world's first ever freefall descent with a manually operated parachute on 28 April 1919. Clear-and-pull from 1500 feet at McCook Airfield, Dayton, Ohio, USA. See *Sky High Irvin* by Peter Hearn (Robert Hale 1983).
Irvin (GB) Ltd	UK parachute manufacturing company founded in 1927 by Leslie Irvin. Irvin Great Britain Ltd., Icknield Way, Letchworth, Herts, SG6 1EU. Tel: 01462 482000.
JM	*See* Jumpmaster.
Jumpmaster	Senior jumper appointed to take charge of parachutists on any particular load. Must be at least FAI 'C' Certificate. (Ops. Manual Section 3).
KAP 3	Old-style Soviet AAD. Barometric or time setting. Springloaded.
Keeper	Metal ring or webbing used to retain control lines on the risers.
Key	FS terminology. Physical or visual signal given to denote completion of one formation (point) and to initiate transition to the next.
Mal.	Parachute malfunction. *See* pp. 47–51.
Manifest	List of jumpers organised by aircraft load. (Ops. Manual 1.3.(b)).
Modification	Design feature of a round canopy which gives forward speed and eliminates

oscillation by directing excess internal air pressure through drive slots.

NCSO	National Coach and Safety Officer.
Net skirt	Mesh band approximately 12 inches deep on the peripheral hem of a round canopy. Introduced in the UK in 1962 by the Irvin Parachute Company on the military PX static line parachute. Designed to prevent blown periphery (line over) type malfunctions.
NOTAM	NOTice to AirMen. Published Air Traffic information; for example, with regard to parachuting activity.
Pad	Electronic target minimum 15cm radius used in Accuracy competition.
PD	Performance Designs. Parachute manufacturer. 1300 E. Int'l Speedway Boulevard, DeLand, Florida 32724 USA. Tel: (1) 904 738 2224.
Piggyback	Type of parachute assembly. Main and reserve mounted in tandem. Cf Front-mounted reserve.
Pilot chute	Small parachute used as a drag device to deploy main canopy. May be hand-deployed or spring-loaded. Also called extractor parachute.
Pin (verb)	Formation Skydiving terminology. To initiate contact with another jumper in freefall. Cf Base.
Pin (noun)	The active jumper in this manoeuvre.
Pin check	Mandatory equipment check carried out on the flight line before emplaning. (Ops. Manual 1.3.(a)). A second pin check may be carried out in the aircraft before exit.
Plain canopy	*See* unmodified canopy.
PLF	Parachute Landing Fall.
Poynter	Daniel F Poynter. US Master Rigger and author of *The Parachute Manual*, the standard work on parachute rigging. Known as the Bible, this is a must for all serious students of the sport. Published by Para

Publishing, PO Box 4232 Santa Barbara, California 93140–4232 USA. Tel: (1) 805 968 7277.

Pull out (Noun)
Pilot chute system in which the container pin is pulled before the pilot chute is released. Cf Throwaway.

QFE
Pressure setting, indicating height above ground datum.

QNH
Pressure setting, indicating altitude above mean sea level.

RAeC
Royal Aero Club. Governing Body of Aviation Sport in the UK. Kimberley House, Vaughan Way, Leicester LE1 4SG. Tel: 0116 253 1051.

RAFSPA
Royal Air Force Sport Parachute Association (Weston on the Green). Tel: 01869 343343.

RAPA
Rhine Army Parachute Association (Bad Lippspringe, Germany). Tel: (49) 05254 98 2378.

RAPS
Ram Air Progression System.

Relative airflow
Flow of air ahead of the aerofoil in the opposite direction to the movement of the ram-air canopy.

Rig
(Sport) parachute assembly.

Rigger
Parachute technician, qualified to repair and manufacture parachute equipment (Ops. Manual Section 14).

Risers
That portion of the suspension system between the lower end of a group of suspension lines and the point of attachment to the load. (*Poynter*).

Rope (slang)
Static line. (USA Dope Rope).

RSL
Reserve Static Line. Short (18 inch) lanyard attached by a shackle to one set of main risers at one end and to the reserve ripcord at the other. The function of the RSL is automatically to deploy the reserve parachute in the event of the main being cut away. Also known as Stevens Lanyard after its inventor, Perry Stevens (USA).

Running	Flying the canopy downwind on full drive.
RW	Relative Work. Freefall exercise involving two or more parachutists flying in contact with or in close proximity to each other. Designated Formation Skydiving as a competition discipline.
Sentinel	Sentinel Mark 2000 pyrotechnic AAD. Withdrawn from the Sport Parachute market in 1987, although many remain in use. Replacement cartridges were still being sold in 1990. Developed and manufactured by SSE Inc.
Series	Combination of turn, turn, loop, turn, turn, loop used in Freefall Style competition.
Set	*See* Series.
Slider	Retardation device used on ram-air canopies to control the opening sequence.
Span	The longitudinal measurement of a wing or ram-air canopy; Cf Chord.
Spot (noun)	The selected exit point. *See* Chapter 6. Also used as a verb.
Squid	High-speed partial malfunction occurring when the critical opening velocity of the parachute is exceeded and the canopy mouth remains closed.
SSE Inc.	Steve Snyder Inc. Developer and manufacturer of ALTIMASTER altimeter series and SENTINEL AADs. 5801 Magnolia Avenue, Pennsauken NJ 08109 USA. Tel: (1) 609 663 2234.
Standoff	High altitude immediate opening, using glide capability of ram-air canopy to cover long distances.
Static line	Line hooked up to strongpoint in aircraft which automatically opens the jumper's parachute. Student jumpers must make a minimum of five static line jumps before progressing to freefall. (Ops. Manual 2.4.).
STC	Safety and Training Committee of the BPA.
Stevens Lanyard	*See* RSL.

Stick	Military parachuting term. Denotes the number of jumpers leaving the aircraft in rapid succession, or that same number on the ground. Originates in RAF terminology *stick* of bombs.
Streamer	High-speed partial malfunction; the canopy elongates and does not inflate.
Style	Individual competition discipline, consisting of left, right and cross series. Designated Freefall Style as a competition event.
T 10	Military static-line parachute (USA).
Tandem	1. Dual harness system which allows an experienced jumper (Tandem master) to carry a passenger in freefall.
	2. Parachute assembly with both main and reserve mounted on a common harness. Same as piggyback.
Telemeters	Tripod-mounted 10 × 80 observation binoculars. Pre-1945 vintage, of German manufacture, their original purpose was anti-aircraft (flak) prediction in WW II.
Terminal	Terminal velocity. Equilibrium freefall speed attained following the initial acceleration phase of about 12 seconds. *See* Table 1.1 on p. 26.
Three ring	Three ring canopy release mechanism invented in 1976 by Bill Booth. The Relative Workshop, 1645 Lexington Avenue, Deland, Florida 32724 USA. Tel: (1) 904 736 7589. Now used worldwide.
Throwaway (Noun)	Pilot chute system in which the container pin is pulled by the drag of the pilot chute. May be positioned on legstrap or BOC. *See* p. 73. (Cf Pullout).
Total	Total malfunction. Container remains closed. *See* p. 48.
Track (noun)	Horizontal movement in freefall. Also verb. *See* p. 70.
TSE	Thomas Sports Equipment. UK equipment manufacturer. Penfold Lane, Bridlington, East Yorkshire YO16 5XS. Tel: 01262 678299.

TSO	Technical Standard Order. FAA regulation that requires certain minimum performance standards and specifications for the certification of a parachute design (*Poynter*).
Unmodified canopy	Non-steerable, usually flat circular, canopy without drive slots. *See* Modification.
USPA	United States Parachute Association. 1440 Duke Street, Alexandria, Virginia 22314 USA. Tel: (1) 703 836 3495.
WARP	Worldwide Approved Relativework Progression. System for teaching Formation Skydiving at Categories 9 and 10.
WDI	Wind Drift Indicator. *See* p. 45.
Wind line	Imaginary line drawn from the opening point through the target to the WDI landing point.
WPC	World Parachuting Championships. The disciplines of Sport Parachuting are:

Freefall Style and Accuracy Landing (Classics)
Formation Skydiving (Relative Work)
Canopy Formation (Canopy Relative Work)
Paraski

WPCs are organised by the International Parachuting Commission of the FAI. Championships at each discipline are held once every two years.

The first WPC organised by the FAI took place in 1954 in St Yan in eastern France. Eight nations were represented, including a team from Great Britain, sponsored by the GQ Parachute Company.

The first British success was achieved in 1968 at the 9th WPC in Graz (Austria) where the team took bronze medals in the Team Accuracy event.

In 1978 at the 14th WPC in Zagreb (former Yugoslavia) Jackie Young of Great Britain won the gold medal in the Individual Accuracy event and in so doing became the first person ever to score 10 consecutive dead centres in 10 rounds at a World Meet.

In 1979 Great Britain took the silver medal in the four-way event at the 3rd World RW (now Formation Skydiving) Championships held at Châteauroux in France. The team was Dane Kenny, Rob Colpus, Will Grut, Geoff Sanders and Jackie Young.

In 1980 Alan (Scotty) Milne took the Individual Accuracy bronze medal at the 15th Style and Accuracy WPC in Kazanlak (Bulgaria).